THE
COMMON COLD

THE ENCYCLOPEDIA OF HEALTH

MEDICAL DISORDERS AND THEIR TREATMENT

Dale C. Garell · General Editor

THE COMMON COLD

Mary Kittredge

Introduction by C. Everett Koop, M.D., Sc.D.
Surgeon General, U.S. Public Health Service

CHELSEA HOUSE PUBLISHERS
New York · Philadelphia

The goal of the ENCYCLOPEDIA OF HEALTH *is to provide general information in the ever-changing areas of physiology, psychology, and related medical issues. The titles in this series are not intended to take the place of the professional advice of a physician or other health-care professional.*

Chelsea House Publishers
EDITOR-IN-CHIEF Nancy Toff
EXECUTIVE EDITOR Remmel T. Nunn
MANAGING EDITOR Karyn Gullen Browne
COPY CHIEF Juliann Barbato
PICTURE EDITOR Adrian G. Allen
ART DIRECTOR Maria Epes
MANUFACTURING MANAGER Gerald Levine

The Encyclopedia of Health
SENIOR EDITOR Paula Edelson

Staff for THE COMMON COLD
ASSISTANT EDITOR Laura Dolce
DEPUTY COPY CHIEF Nicole Bowen
EDITORIAL ASSISTANT Navorn Johnson
PICTURE RESEARCHER Georganne Backman
ASSISTANT ART DIRECTOR Loraine Machlin
SENIOR DESIGNER Marjorie Zaum
DESIGN ASSISTANT Debora Lynfield-Smith
PRODUCTION COORDINATOR Joseph Romano

First Printing

1 3 5 7 9 8 6 4 2

Library of Congress Cataloging-in-Publication Data

Kittredge, Mary, 1949–
    The Common Cold / Mary Kittredge; introduction by C. Everett Koop.
    p. cm. — (The Encyclopedia of health. Medical disorders and their treatment)
    Bibliography: p.
    Includes index.
    Summary: Explains the common cold, including symptoms, causes, treatments, and prevention.
    ISBN 0-7910-0060-5
         0-7910-0487-2 (pbk.)
    1. Cold (Disease)—Juvenile literature. [1. Cold (Disease)]
I. Title. II. Series.   89-10009
RF361.K58 1990   CIP
616.2′05–dc20   AC

CONTENTS

THE ENCYCLOPEDIA OF
H E A L T H

THE HEALTHY BODY

The Circulatory System
Dental Health
The Digestive System
The Endocrine System
Exercise
Genetics & Heredity
The Human Body: An Overview
Hygiene
The Immune System
Memory & Learning
The Musculoskeletal System
The Neurological System
Nutrition
The Reproductive System
The Respiratory System
The Senses
Speech & Hearing
Sports Medicine
Vision
Vitamins & Minerals

THE LIFE CYCLE

Adolescence
Adulthood
Aging
Childhood
Death & Dying
The Family
Friendship & Love
Pregnancy & Birth

MEDICAL ISSUES

Careers in Health Care
Environmental Health
Folk Medicine
Health Care Delivery
Holistic Medicine
Medical Ethics
Medical Fakes & Frauds
Medical Technology
Medicine & the Law
Occupational Health
Public Health

PSYCHOLOGICAL DISORDERS AND THEIR TREATMENT

Anxiety & Phobias
Child Abuse
Compulsive Behavior
Delinquency & Criminal Behavior
Depression
Diagnosing & Treating Mental Illness
Eating Habits & Disorders
Learning Disabilities
Mental Retardation
Personality Disorders
Schizophrenia
Stress Management
Suicide

MEDICAL DISORDERS AND THEIR TREATMENT

AIDS
Allergies
Alzheimer's Disease
Arthritis
Birth Defects
Cancer
The Common Cold
Diabetes
First Aid & Emergency Medicine
Gynecological Disorders
Headaches
The Hospital
Kidney Disorders
Medical Diagnosis
The Mind-Body Connection
Mononucleosis and Other Infectious Diseases
Nuclear Medicine
Organ Transplants
Pain
Physical Handicaps
Poisons & Toxins
Prescription & OTC Drugs
Sexually Transmitted Diseases
Skin Disorders
Stroke & Heart Disease
Substance Abuse
Tropical Medicine

PREVENTION AND EDUCATION: THE KEYS TO GOOD HEALTH

C. Everett Koop, M.D., Sc.D.
Surgeon General,
U.S. Public Health Service

The issue of health education has received particular attention in recent years because of the presence of AIDS in the news. But our response to this particular tragedy points up a number of broader issues that doctors, public health officials, educators, and the public face. In particular, it points up the necessity for sound health education for citizens of all ages.

Over the past 25 years this country has been able to bring about dramatic declines in the death rates for heart disease, stroke, accidents, and, for people under the age of 45, cancer. Today, Americans generally eat better and take better care of themselves than ever before. Thus, with the help of modern science and technology, they have a better chance of surviving serious—even catastrophic—illnesses. That's the good news.

But, like every phonograph record, there's a flip side, and one with special significance for young adults. According to a report issued in 1979 by Dr. Julius Richmond, my predecessor as Surgeon General, Americans aged 15 to 24 had a higher death rate in 1979 than they did 20 years earlier. The causes: violent death and injury, alcohol and drug abuse, unwanted pregnancies, and sexually transmitted diseases. Adolescents are particularly vulnerable, because they are beginning to explore their own sexuality and perhaps to experiment with drugs. The need for educating young people is critical, and the price of neglect is high.

Yet even for the population as a whole, our health is still far from what it could be. Why? A 1974 Canadian government report attributed all death and disease to four broad elements: inadequacies in the health-care system, behavioral factors or unhealthy life-styles, environmental hazards, and human biological factors.

To be sure, there are diseases that are still beyond the control of even our advanced medical knowledge and techniques. And despite yearnings that are as old as the human race itself, there is no "fountain of youth" to ward off aging and death. Still, there is a solution to many of the problems that undermine sound health. In a word, that solution is prevention. Prevention, which includes health promotion and education, saves lives, improves the quality of life, and, in the long run, saves money.

In the United States, organized public health activities and preventive medicine have a long history. Important milestones include the improvement of sanitary procedures and the development of pasteurized milk in the late 19th century, and the introduction in the mid-20th century of effective vaccines against polio, measles, German measles, mumps, and other once-rampant diseases. Internationally, organized public health efforts began on a wide-scale basis with the International Sanitary Conference of 1851, to which 12 nations sent representatives. The World Health Organization, founded in 1948, continues these efforts under the aegis of the United Nations, with particular emphasis on combatting communicable diseases and the training of health-care workers.

But despite these accomplishments, much remains to be done in the field of prevention. For too long, we have had a medical care system that is science- and technology-based, focused, essentially, on illness and mortality. It is now patently obvious that both the social and the economic costs of such a system are becoming insupportable.

Implementing prevention—and its corollaries, health education and promotion—is the job of several groups of people:

First, the medical and scientific professions need to continue basic scientific research, and here we are making considerable progress. But increased concern with prevention will also have a decided impact on how primary-care doctors practice medicine. With a shift to health-based rather than morbidity-based medicine, the role of the "new physician" will include a healthy dose of patient education.

Second, practitioners of the social and behavioral sciences—psychologists, economists, city planners—along with lawyers, business leaders, and government officials—must solve the practical and ethical dilemmas confronting us: poverty, crime, civil rights, literacy, education, employment, housing, sanitation, environmental protection, health care delivery systems, and so forth. All of these issues affect public health.

Third is the public at large. We'll consider that very important group in a moment.

Fourth, and the linchpin in this effort, is the public health profession—doctors, epidemiologists, teachers—who must harness the professional expertise of the first two groups and the common sense and cooperation of the third, the public. They must define the problems statistically and qualitatively and then help us set priorities for finding the solutions.

To a very large extent, improving those statistics is the responsibility of every individual. So let's consider more specifically what the role of the individual should be and why health education is so important to that role. First, and most obviously, individuals can protect themselves from illness and injury and thus minimize their need for professional medical care. They can eat a nutritious diet, get adequate exercise, avoid tobacco, alcohol, and drugs, and take prudent steps to avoid accidents. The proverbial "apple a day keeps the doctor away" is not so far from the truth, after all.

Second, individuals should actively participate in their own medical care. They should schedule regular medical and dental checkups. Should they develop an illness or injury, they should know when to treat themselves and when to seek professional help. To gain the maximum benefit from any medical treatment that they do require, individuals must become partners in that treatment. For instance, they should understand the effects and side effects of medications. I counsel young physicians that there is no such thing as too much information when talking with patients. But the corollary is the patient must know enough about the nuts and bolts of the healing process to understand what the doctor is telling him. That is at least partially the patient's responsibility.

Education is equally necessary for us to understand the ethical and public policy issues in health care today. Sometimes individuals will encounter these issues in making decisions about their own treatment or that of family members. Other citizens may encounter them as jurors in medical malpractice cases. But we all become involved, indirectly, when we elect our public officials, from school board members to the president. Should surrogate parenting be legal? To what extent is drug testing desirable, legal, or necessary? Should there be public funding for family planning, hospitals, various types of medical research, and medical care for the indigent? How should we allocate scant technological resources, such as kidney dialysis and organ transplants? What is the proper role of government in protecting the rights of patients?

What are the broad goals of public health in the United States today? In 1980, the Public Health Service issued a report aptly entitled *Promoting Health-Preventing Disease: Objectives for the Nation.* This report expressed its goals in terms of mortality and in terms of intermediate goals in education and health improvement. It identified 15 major concerns: controlling high blood pressure; improving family planning; improving pregnancy care and infant health; increasing the rate of immunization; controlling sexually transmitted diseases; controlling the presence of toxic agents and radiation in the environment; improving occupational safety and health; preventing accidents; promoting water fluoridation and dental health; controlling infectious diseases; decreasing smoking; decreasing alcohol and drug abuse; improving nutrition; promoting physical fitness and exercise; and controlling stress and violent behavior.

For healthy adolescents and young adults (ages 15 to 24), the specific goal was a 20% reduction in deaths, with a special focus on motor vehicle injuries and alcohol and drug abuse. For adults (ages 25 to 64), the aim was 25% fewer deaths, with a concentration on heart attacks, strokes, and cancers.

Smoking is perhaps the best example of how individual behavior can have a direct impact on health. Today cigarette smoking is recognized as the most important single preventable cause of death in our society. It is responsible for more cancers and more cancer deaths than any other known agent; is a prime risk factor for heart and blood vessel disease, chronic bronchitis, and emphysema; and is a frequent cause of complications in pregnancies and of babies born prematurely, underweight, or with potentially fatal respiratory and cardiovascular problems.

Since the release of the Surgeon General's first report on smoking in 1964, the proportion of adult smokers has declined substantially, from 43% in 1965 to 30.5% in 1985. Since 1965, 37 million people have quit smoking. Although there is still much work to be done if we are to become a "smoke-free society," it is heartening to note that public health and public education efforts—such as warnings on cigarette packages and bans on broadcast advertising—have already had significant effects.

In 1835, Alexis de Tocqueville, a French visitor to America, wrote, "In America the passion for physical well-being is general." Today, as then, health and fitness are front-page items. But with the greater scientific and technological resources now available to us, we are in a far stronger position to make good health care available to everyone. And with the greater technological threats to us as we approach the 21st century, the need to do so is more urgent than ever before. Comprehensive information about basic biology, preventive medicine, medical and surgical treatments, and related ethical and public policy issues can help you arm yourself with the knowledge you need to be healthy throughout your life.

FOREWORD

Dale C. Garell, M.D.

A dvances in our understanding of health and disease during the 20th century have been truly remarkable. Indeed, it could be argued that modern health care is one of the greatest accomplishments in all of human history. In the early 1900s, improvements in sanitation, water treatment, and sewage disposal reduced death rates and increased longevity. Previously untreatable illnesses can now be managed with antibiotics, immunizations, and modern surgical techniques. Discoveries in the fields of immunology, genetic diagnosis, and organ transplantation are revolutionizing the prevention and treatment of disease. Modern medicine is even making inroads against cancer and heart disease, two of the leading causes of death in the United States.

Although there is much to be proud of, medicine continues to face enormous challenges. Science has vanquished diseases such as smallpox and polio, but new killers, most notably AIDS, confront us. Moreover, we now victimize ourselves with what some have called "diseases of choice," or those brought on by drug and alcohol abuse, bad eating habits, and mismanagement of the stresses and strains of contemporary life. The very technology that is doing so much to prolong life has brought with it previously unimaginable ethical dilemmas related to issues of death and dying. The rising cost of health-care is a matter of central concern to us all. And violence in the form of automobile accidents, homicide, and suicide remain the major killers of young adults.

In the past, most people were content to leave health care and medical treatment in the hands of professionals. But since the 1960s, the consumer of medical care—that is, the patient—has assumed an increasingly central role in the management of his or her own health. There has also been a new emphasis placed on prevention: People are recognizing that their own actions can help prevent many of the conditions that have caused death and disease in the past. This accounts for the growing commitment to good nutrition and regular exercise, for the fact that more and more people are choosing not to smoke, and for a new moderation in people's drinking habits.

People want to know more about themselves and their own health. They are curious about their body: its anatomy, physiology, and biochemistry. They want to keep up with rapidly evolving medical technologies and procedures. They are willing to educate themselves about common disorders and diseases so that they can be full partners in their own health-care.

The ENCYCLOPEDIA OF HEALTH is designed to provide the basic knowledge that readers will need if they are to take significant responsibility for their own health. It is also meant to serve as a frame of reference for further study and exploration. The ENCYCLOPEDIA is divided into five subsections: The Healthy Body; The Life Cycle; Medical Disorders & Their Treatment; Psychological Disorders & Their Treatment; and Medical Issues. For each topic covered by the ENCYCLOPEDIA, we present the essential facts about the relevant biology; the symptoms, diagnosis, and treatment of common diseases and disorders; and ways in which you can prevent or reduce the severity of health problems when that is possible. The ENCYCLOPEDIA also projects what may lie ahead in the way of future treatment or prevention strategies.

The broad range of topics and issues covered in the ENCYCLOPEDIA reflects the fact that human health encompasses physical, psychological, social, environmental, and spiritual well-being. Just as the mind and the body are inextricably linked, so, too, is the individual an integral part of the wider world that comprises his or her family, society, and environment. To discuss health in its broadest aspect it is necessary to explore the many ways in which it is connected to such fields as law, social science, public policy, economics, and even religion. And so, the ENCYCLOPEDIA is meant to be a bridge between science, medical technology, the world at large, and you. I hope that it will inspire you to pursue in greater depth particular areas of interest, and that you will take advantage of the suggestions for further reading and the lists of resources and organizations that can provide additional information.

AUTHOR'S PREFACE

Human beings have made more progress against more kinds of illness in the 20th century alone than in all the earlier centuries combined. Diseases such as polio, typhoid fever, malaria, and even some heart diseases and cancers—all of which have wiped out millions of people in the past—are today among

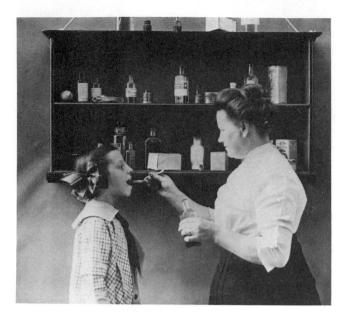

An early-20th-century photograph of a mother giving cough syrup to her daughter. With or without treatment, most colds go away by themselves in about seven days.

the many ailments that medical science can treat and often even cure. Yet there is a "minor" ailment that, despite the remarkable advances of medicine, remains incurable: the common cold.

At this very minute, in fact, close to 5% of all Americans—around 12 million people—have colds. Most people catch from one to six colds every year. On any given day, about 1 of 4 children in day-care centers has a cold, and perhaps 1 of 20 readers of this book is suffering cold symptoms right now, even while reading about them.

In fact, almost everyone has endured a cold at one time or another: the scratchy throat, cough and sneezing, aches and fever that are the usual miseries of the illness. Most young people have felt the disappointment of missing a school or social event because of a bad cold and more than once have had to put up with the red, runny nose, the congestion, and the "wiped out" feeling a common cold can inflict. Many young people know too that time is the only sure cure: Untreated, almost every cold will run its course and go away by itself in about seven days. Most people also know that the majority of colds are not serious: The common cold rarely leads to anything worse, and it rarely leaves permanent ill effects.

Many people do not know, however, that some of the effects of this "minor" ailment are anything but mild: Common colds cause 70 million lost work or school days per year in the United

States, and victims spend about $5 billion on cold treatments—
$3 billion on visits to doctors and clinics and $2 billion on drugs
and other kinds of remedies. Colds can lead to serious diseases,
too, for although a cold itself is not usually dangerous, its complications (especially when the cold is neglected) can include ear,
throat, and sinus infections, bronchitis, and even pneumonia. In
short, colds cost money, cause suffering, waste time, and may
sometimes lead to serious ailments.

Colds are among medicine's most stubborn mysteries. Why do
boys catch more colds than girls among children under age four,
whereas after the age of four girls catch more? And—perhaps
the most tantalizing question of all—will an effective prevention
or cure for this mystifying ailment ever be found?

An engraving depicting
the Great Plague of
1665 in London. While
many such deadly dis-
eases have been eradi-
cated, medical science
has not yet found either
a cure or a vaccine for
the common cold.

THE PLAGUE OF LONDON 1665.

Answers to these and other questions about colds lie in the still-undiscovered secrets of the human immune system—the body's powerful and complex disease-fighting machinery—and in the secrets of cold-causing germs called viruses, infectious agents hundreds of times smaller than bacteria. The search for a true cold cure is helping to uncover knowledge about the immune system and about viruses of all kinds—knowledge that may eventually lead to a treatment not only for the common cold but for other, more serious ailments as well.

At this time there is no cure for a cold: no prescription drug against the viruses that cause it and no over-the-counter remedy that does more than ease its symptoms. Does this mean that there is nothing that can be done about the common cold?

Not at all. Despite the lack of drugs to fight directly against the viruses that cause colds, there is knowledge regarding what can be done when such viruses attack. So although colds cannot yet be prevented or cured, this knowledge can enable people to suffer less and spend less money when battling them. Most of the possibly serious complications of colds, too, can be guarded against by learning their symptoms and taking proper measures against them. Knowledge, in fact, may be the most potent weapon against the common cold.

In one recent study reported in the *Journal of the American Medical Association* in October 1983, visits to doctors for cold symptoms were reduced more than 40% when health clinics simply gave facts about colds to patients. Informed patients spent less money on doctors and cold medicines, suffered less anxiety about their illnesses, and had no more complications from their colds than people who visited a doctor each time they developed cold symptoms. Until a true cure for the common cold is found, then, knowledge about the disease is the key to preventing it when possible and to enduring it as safely and comfortably as possible when prevention efforts are not successful.

•   •   •   •

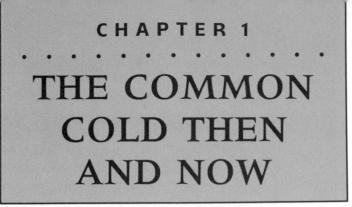

CHAPTER 1

. . . .

THE COMMON COLD THEN AND NOW

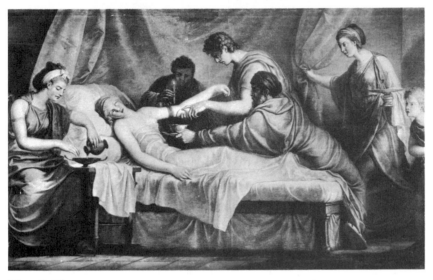

Bloodletting.

Throughout the history of civilization, people have been catching colds, trying to understand how and why they caught them, and trying—without very much success—to get rid of them.

As early as 3,000 years ago, the Chinese found that tea made from the bushy shrub called *mahuang* relieved a stuffy nose. The active ingredient in their herbal remedy was *ephedrine*, one of the earliest known effective drugs. In fact, its synthetic equivalent, *pseudoephedrine*, is widely used in commercial cold remedies today.

The Greek physician Hippocrates (ca. 460–ca. 377 B.C.) believed that colds were caused by too much waste matter in the brain. He believed the runny nose of a cold represented the overflow of this waste matter, so he called the common cold *catarrh*, for the Greek word meaning "flow." (The English word *catarrh* still means a cold with a runny nose.)

Hippocrates' fellow physicians prescribed bloodletting—either by cutting the sufferer's flesh or by applying bloodsucking leeches—to rid the body more quickly of the excess fluid. Although Hippocrates did not believe in the healing powers of bloodletting, the practice became a standard method for treatment of colds and other illnesses. Called leeching, it continued to be practiced in many parts of the world at least until the latter half of the 19th century.

Bloodletting was not, however, the only remedy people tried for relief of the common cold. In Rome, the scholar Pliny the Elder (A.D. 23–79) recommended kissing the furry nose of a mouse to cure sneezing and coughs caused by the common cold. Twelfth-century philosopher and physician Maimonides of Egypt thought soup from a fat hen was a sure cure for the disease, and chicken soup is still a commonly used remedy today.

An ancient cure called dry cupping also remains popular, especially in parts of Asia and South America. The method consists of placing jars that have been heated by candles or still contain burning candles on the cold sufferer's back in hopes of drawing out the toxins that caused the cold. In fact, the warm, stinging sensation thus produced does not cure colds, but it probably does distract the victim from his or her common-cold symptoms for a while.

During the Middle Ages in Europe, the Catholic church, which considered some cold symptoms to be warnings of evil to come or of demons trying to invade the body, recommended prayer as a treatment. Sneezing was considered an especially bad sign because people thought that during a sneeze the soul could leave the body and a demon take its place. Covering the mouth while sneezing was said to block the invading spirit; saying "God bless you" when someone else sneezed kept demons away, too. Among the cold cures and preventives of the Middle Ages were garlic necklaces (also believed effective against demons, werewolves, and vampires), collars made of salted herring (to keep evil influences from the throat), and sandwiches of the victims' hair fed to village dogs. This last remedy was based on the idea that cut pieces of hair, taken away from the owner's body, would "draw off" the cold.

An early American student of colds, their causes, and their cures was Benjamin Franklin, the 18th-century statesman and scientist. Franklin did not agree with the idea still believed to be true by many people that getting chilled or wet would cause one, to catch a cold. "I have suffered Cold to an Extremity only short of Freezing, but this did not make me catch Cold. I have been in the River every Evening for 2 or 3 hours," wrote Franklin, who swam each day for exercise, "and One should suppose that I have had enough Damp to take Cold if Humidity could give it. But A Body filled with Watery Fluids from Head to Foot cannot be hurt by a little Addition of Moisture."

Franklin also came very close to guessing the true cause of colds. They were the result, he said, of "animal Substances in perspired Matter from our Bodies, passed by the Air. People catch Colds when . . . near each other so as to breathe each other's Transpiration [exhaled breath]." Franklin had his own cold-prevention method, too: breathing plenty of fresh air. When he shared a room with future American president John Adams one night in 1776, he insisted on sleeping with the windows open, and when Adams protested that the frigid night air would give them both a cold, Franklin gave Adams a speech on the true cause and prevention of the disease—a speech so long and boring, Adams later wrote, that he fell asleep in spite of the chilly breeze blowing over his bed.

It was not until the late 1800s, however, that Franklin's remarkably accurate ideas on colds began to receive scientific backing. Scientists were first able to observe bacteria in 1683 under a microscope invented by Dutch scientist Antonie van Leeuwenhoek. Two centuries later, in 1898, another Dutch scientist, botanist Martinus Beijerinck, was filtering bacteria from a plant-juice solution when he noticed something strange. An organism

Panaceas, Potions, and Elixirs

In the early part of the 20th century, hundreds of medicines were developed to cure all of mankind's ailments. Many of these cure-alls were designed to fight a number of illnesses or symptoms, including the common cold. Few of these panaceas had any medicinal value, however, and many actually contained powerful narcotic drugs. The advertisements shown on these two pages are representative of those for elixirs sold at the time to treat the common cold.

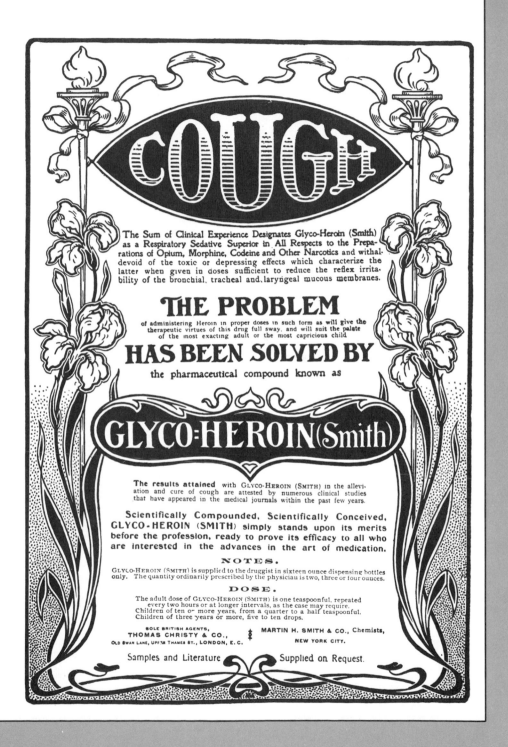

too small to be stopped by his fine bacteria-filter was ruining his experiments. He could not see the tiny, destructive organism, even through a microscope, but its effects made him certain that it did exist. He called the new organism a virus, from the Latin word *virus*, meaning "a slimy or poisonous substance."

At the same time, rising enthusiasm over many kinds of scientific advances helped fuel a demand for patent medicines and medical devices to "scientifically cure" a large number of ailments, including colds. Thus, in 19th-century America, many people turned away from the mystical cures and homemade medicines of their ancestors in favor of pills, tonics, potions, and powders sold in drugstores and by traveling "medicine men." Some products were relatively mild; the Kickapoo Indian Cure-All ("Safe and Effective for Man or Beast") contained only rum and molasses, for example. Some contained useless herbs but vastly inflated claims for their effectiveness were made, such as those made for Dr. R. V. Pierce's Golden Medical Discovery. It was said to give "immediate and permanent cure for every respiratory disease," and the claim was made that whoever took the potion would "feel like a perfect being."

Other patent medicines, such as the Tyler Cherokee Remedy, contained potent narcotic drugs, including morphine, heroin, and cocaine. Panaceas, or cure-alls, such as these were legal to sell and take because at that time no laws regulated habit-forming substances and, indeed, little was known about the addictive properties of these drugs. The Tyler remedy and similar nostrums claimed to cure colds, coughs, asthma, and even tuberculosis, but the medicines' real effect was to make people too drug intoxicated to notice the symptoms of their ailments. Narcotic-based remedies made drug addicts of many people who took them until 1914, when Congress passed the Harrison Act to regulate the sale of narcotics.

Just as popular as patent medicines were the various devices advertised to cure colds: Among these were nasal sprays to squirt sea water, herb teas, or cocaine-based remedies into the nostrils; and jars filled with mint leaves, camphorated oil, and other "congestion relievers" that when heated released "healing fumes" that sufferers breathed through tubes or face masks. Few of these devices did any good, but one that did really help people was the

A makeshift vaporizer. Throughout the centuries, thousands of medicines, potions, and devices have been invented to ease the discomfort associated with the common cold. For the most part, however, these "cures" have been ineffective.

steam-mist vaporizer. The vaporizer humidified the air and thus helped broken skin in nasal passages heal, helped liquefy mucus so it could be coughed out, and in general made cold victims feel better. When kept clean according to manufacturer's instructions, it is still used to good effect today.

The 19th century saw the discovery of another effective cold-treating device when, in 1830, *salicylic acid* (a substance found in willow bark, used for hundreds of years to reduce pain and fever when made into a tea) was synthesized in the laboratory of the German company Bayer Pharmaceuticals. The new drug, *acetylsalicylic acid*, swiftly became available in products such as Bayer Aspirin (Bayer originally coined the term *aspirin* for ace-

A medicine man sells his wares on the streets of London in this 1876 photo. Many of these "quacks" sold potions laced with alcohol or narcotic drugs.

tylsalicylic acid and used it as a trademark for a number of years) and Bromo Seltzer. Many people use aspirin to combat the aches and fever of the common cold.

It should be noted, however, that in the 1970s scientists confirmed that aspirin increases the risk of a serious, potentially fatal complication of viral illnesses. This malady, known as *Reye's syndrome*, affects children and young adults. For this reason, the American Academy of Pediatrics recommends that children and teenagers avoid taking aspirin during and after viral illnesses, including colds. Instead, they should use *acetaminophen* (the active ingredient in such medications as Tylenol), a drug similar in its pain-relieving properties to aspirin but without the potential side effects.

The 20th century brought with it the beginnings of true knowledge about the cause of the common cold. In 1914, German scientist V. W. Kruse showed that material from the noses of people suffering colds, when filtered clean of bacteria, could still cause colds when put into healthy people's noses. For a while it was thought that such material contained *toxins*—poisons produced by bacteria—and that toxins caused cold symptoms. But analysis showed that the substances contained no toxins, so scientists began to believe that viruses must be the culprit.

The development of the electron microscope (a microscope in which electrons are bounced off particles too small to see with a regular microscope and then rebound onto film, which is then developed) in 1939 finally enabled researchers to see viruses. In

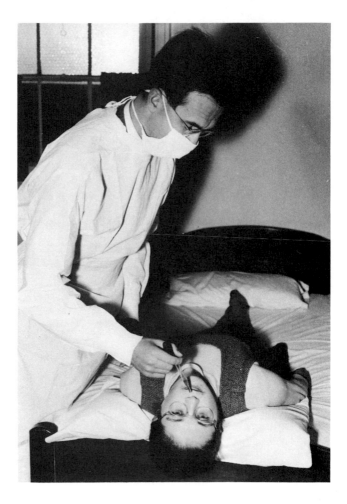

Dr. D. A. Tyrrell, a virologist at the Harvard Common Cold Research Center in Salisbury, England, puts drops of the common-cold virus into a volunteer's nose in 1958.

The Many Faces of a Cold

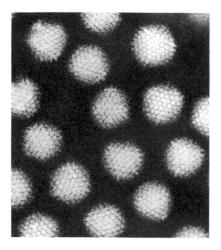

The adenovirus (left) and the coxsackie virus (below) are just two of the many viruses that cause the common cold. Because there are so many different viruses that cause colds, the search for a vaccine and a cure has been largely unsuccessful.

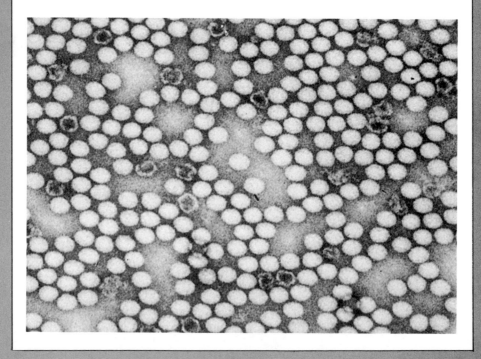

1949, scientist John Enders of the Boston Children's Hospital found a way of growing viruses in the laboratory—a feat that won him the Nobel Prize in Medicine in 1954 and paved the way for Albert Sabin's development of a vaccine against the poliovirus a few years later, as well as for vast advances in the area of cold research.

In 1955, cold-researcher Sir Christopher Andrewes of the Common Cold Research Unit in Salisbury, England, confirmed the identification of one virus that definitely did cause colds. Once this virus was found, Andrewes and others thought a cold vaccine—a preventive medicine against common colds—must be very near. Scientific hopes were soon dashed, however, when many more cold viruses were isolated. Worse, many were of different species—still viruses, but different from one another in important ways. By the early 1960s, dozens of cold viruses had been isolated; in the 1980s, the number had reached 200 and was still growing. That, as Andrewes realized in 1955, means a cold vaccine may be nearly impossible to develop, because a vaccine works only against one specific virus; to create one that works against 200 or more disease agents is far beyond the ability of present-day science.

Meanwhile, research in the late 20th century continues to disprove old theories and suggest new ideas about colds: Once believed to spread mostly by coughs and sneezes, these illnesses are now thought to pass from person to person more frequently by hand, as people touch virus-contaminated objects and then touch their eyes, mouth, or nose. An increasing number of people now believe that nonphysical factors, such as emotional stress, also seem to alter people's chances of catching colds. The human body's immune system—its defense against colds and other illnesses and diseases—has come under intense study because of the recent development of serious diseases such as AIDS (acquired immune deficiency syndrome), a fatal disease of the immune system spread by exposure to contaminated body fluids, usually through the sharing of infected needles by drug addicts and through sexual contact between an infected and a noninfected person. Finally, research on colds and other viral illnesses has led to developments that may prove useful for their prevention or treatment: Among the newest potential weapons against virus-borne diseases are a synthetic version of *interferon*, one of the body's natural disease-fighting substances, and a laboratory-made virus-blocking particle, the *monoclonal antibody*.

Until a cure can be found, colds continue to be a common problem for almost everyone. And because cure or prevention of the common cold might pave the way for progress against other virus-caused ailments, too, the search for a victory against colds goes on with undiminished energy.

•   •   •   •

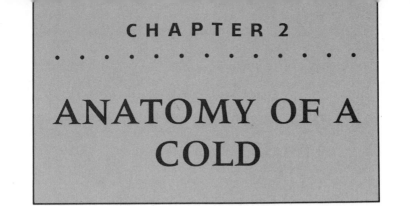

CHAPTER 2

. . . .

ANATOMY OF A COLD

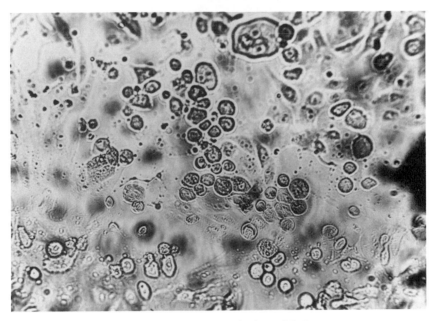

A microphotograph of cells infected with the cold virus.

The common cold is an illness that occurs when viruses invade the human nose and throat. As previously mentioned, there are at least 200 known species of cold-causing viruses. Although there is such a large number of these, cold viruses and other viruses are all alike in a number of important ways. First, viruses are extremely small. A typical virus is only about 1/100,000 of an inch long. Some are even smaller—almost as tiny as a billionth of an inch. Second, most viruses are shaped either like rods or like multisided domes.

Another characteristic viruses have in common is that they are primitive. Even one-celled creatures such as bacteria have structures for taking in food, turning it into energy, and giving off waste, but viruses do not. Instead, each individual virus particle, or *virion*, consists simply of an outer protein coat, called a *capsid*, which surrounds the *nucleoid*, one or two strands of DNA or RNA. DNA (deoxyribonucleic acid) and RNA (ribonucleic acid) are the molecules that contain hereditary information: in this case, instructions for making more viruses. Some viruses may also have a tail structure that helps them attach to the cells they infect.

Viruses share some characteristics with both the living and the nonliving. Like living organisms, they can reproduce, but they can do so only within a living cell. Viruses do not eat, breathe, grow, repair injuries, or give off waste. This makes them different from all living things; in fact, if they did not reproduce, viruses would probably be clearly classified as nonliving.

Although viruses are small, simple parasites (creatures that parasites live in are called the parasites' *hosts*), they are not weak. Freezing temperatures and lack of oxygen cannot kill them, and forces of up to 100,000 times Earth's gravity cannot crush them. They can survive in the air, under water, or in deep space, and even strong chemicals designed to destroy them may take hours to overwhelm their tough outer coat. Some viruses may exist for hundreds of years without finding a host to infect, and the waiting does them no harm. When they do find a host, they begin instantly doing the one thing viruses can do: invading the host's cells in order to reproduce inside of them.

Common-cold viruses may reach cells in the human nose and throat after traveling from the outer part of the nose or from the moist membranes of the eye via the tear duct. Or they may enter by being inhaled with tiny moisture droplets—from the sneeze of an infected person, for instance. Cold viruses that enter the body cannot infect cells at once, however; they must first get past the body's outer defenses against them.

The body's first defense against cold viruses is the nose. Hairs in the nose trap foreign matter, such as dust or tiny water droplets, which may be carrying viruses. A coating of thin mucus acts as a shield for the skin deeper within the nose. Also, because viruses breed best in cold, dry air, the inside of the nose is warmed and humidified by a rich blood supply near the surface of the skin. Flaplike ridges called *turbinates* increase the warming and humidifying process. So even very cold, dry air warms to body temperature and moistens to about 75% humidity as it passes through the nose.

Viruses that reach the back of the nose and the upper throat face another barrier. Cells here produce a substance called *immunoglobulin A*, or IgA, which blocks viruses from invading them. Immunoglobulin A is one of five types of immunoglobulins. Immunoglobulins are antibodies—germ-fighting proteins. In order to understand how these immunoglobulins work, it is first necessary to understand how a virus invades a cell. In order to invade a cell, a virus must first attach itself to the cell's surface.

Viruses that pass into the nasal cavity are often caught up by nasal hair and mucus (left) and sneezed out. Viruses that get past the nose are often trapped in the mucus lining the throat passage and held by the cilia (right) until they are either swallowed or coughed out.

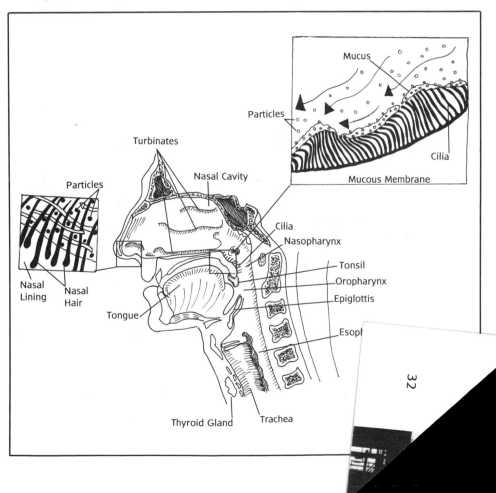

To do so, it must fit into a specially shaped attachment point on the cell, like a piece in a jigsaw puzzle. Immunoglobulin A prevents this from taking place by attaching itself to the virus in the spot at which the virus would have attached to the cell, thus filling the bonding site.

A virus that does, by chance, get past the upper throat may reach the *trachea*, the main air tube leading into the lungs. Here the virus faces a sticky mucous layer and a swarm of tiny hairs called *cilia*. The cilia send the mucous coat steadily back up toward the throat at a speed of about one inch every five minutes. Once a virus trapped in the mucus travels back up to the throat, it is swallowed and destroyed by acids in the stomach.

If the viruses' intended victim is in good general health, the body's defenses may stop these invading organisms at this point—before they can reach their target cells. But a person who is weakened by another illness or whose defense mechanisms have been damaged—by smoking, air pollution, or allergies, for example—may not be able to ward off a viral invasion. Even healthy defenses cannot win every cold battle at this early stage.

Viruses that penetrate the body's first defenses home in on their main targets: those cells that line the nose and throat, or

Although the body is equipped with its own system for fighting off colds, a person whose defense system is weakened or damaged by illness or air pollution may not be able to ward off a viral infection.

epithelial cells. Hours after entering the body, the viruses attach by the hundreds of thousands to the target cells' surfaces. Sensing the viruses' presence, each target cell "puckers up," surrounds the virus, and sucks it in, in an attempt to engulf and destroy the invader. But instead of destroying them, the effort merely brings the viruses inside the target cells—just the place they were trying to reach from the start. (Some viruses are so aggressive that they do not wait to be surrounded; instead they punch holes in the target cells to get inside.)

An invaded cell tries to destroy its enemy, dissolving the virus's capsid with strong chemicals in an attempt to disintegrate it. But this also helps the virus, for with its capsid outer coat dissolved its nucleoid, DNA or RNA, is free inside the cell.

Meanwhile, the invaded cell has its own DNA, instructions telling it how to produce more cells just like itself. But unlike the virus, the cell also has mechanisms—structures called ribosomes that follow DNA instructions—and raw materials to use in cellular reproduction. When a virus invades a cell, it substitutes its own DNA instructions for the ones belonging to the cell, then takes over all the cell's equipment and raw materials. Now the virus will force the cell to produce new viruses.

A virus can be transmitted by dishes, toys, or books that an infected person has touched.

See a Doctor If

- Cold symptoms last more than a week (this may be a sign of allergy).

- Persistent pain develops in the ears, glands, neck, or sinuses.

- A sore throat persists for a full week or is accompanied either by a fever that stays over 100° for 48 hours or at 101° for 24 hours.

- A sore throat is severe and accompanied by an earache.

- A cough lasts more than 10 days or is accompanied by a fever over 102°.

- Mucus is very thick and/or yellowish, rusty, or green in color.

- Any blood is coughed up.

- Cough is accompanied by sharp chest pain.

- Deep breathing is difficult.

- Shortness of breath persists for more than 48 hours.

- Temperature rises over 103° or remains above 100° for 3 days.

- Any fever lasts over a week.

- Dizziness is accompanied by a fever higher than 102° or a 101° fever that persists for more than 36 hours.

- Dizziness is severe or lasts longer than 36 hours.

- Headache persists more than 48 hours after the fever is gone or is accompanied by visual disturbances.

Reprinted from *Healthfacts*, Center for Consumer Research

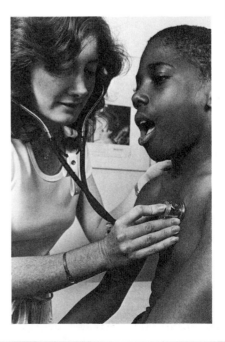

In the first stage of the takeover, part of the viral DNA shuts down the cell's reproduction. As early as 12 hours after cold viruses have successfully invaded, the reproduction centers of 900,000 nose and throat cells have been taken over and shut off.

Next, the viruses start the cells' equipment up again, only now the cells' ribosomes follow the viruses' DNA instructions to make nucleoids for new cold viruses. In half a day this part of the work is done, and the manufacture of the viral capsid begins. The final step—assembly of new virus individuals, or virions—occurs shortly thereafter. Each host cell can make several new virions.

Twenty-four hours after the virus has first invaded the nose and throat cells, the 1 million or so infected cells have been forced to make 90 million more virus individuals—new viruses that can invade other cells and begin the whole cycle anew. To escape from the cell where they were made, new viruses bore holes in the cell's membrane, killing the cell in a process called *lysis.*

By about the second day of a cold, lysis has killed as many as 1 million cells in the nose and throat. Dead cells pile up, and the body attempts to wash them away by secreting a thin, watery fluid from the nose. This is why one early cold symptom is a slight runny nose. The sufferer may also have a faint scratchy throat as the epithelial cells in this area begin dying in significant numbers. Also by now (or earlier, depending on which virus species is the culprit), the cold is contagious: Other people can catch it, even though the symptoms may be so mild that the first victim does not know he or she is infected.

In order for a cold to spread between people, viruses must leave the body of an infected person and enter the body of an uninfected person. They can do so because when the virus population gets large, not only the body's cells but the fluid in the victim's eyes, nose, and throat contain virions. Touching the nose or eyes carries viruses to the fingertips, which may then deposit them on books, toys, or anything else the victim touches. Dishes, towels, bedding, and any other items a victim uses may get a dose of virus, too—a dose the next person can receive by touching the contaminated object, then touching the eyes or nose with virus-laden hands. The process of releasing virus from the body is called *viral shedding* and may begin as early as seven hours after the virus first enters the original victim.

By about the third day of a cold, though, the victim cannot

help but notice some symptoms: itchy eyes, runny nose, sneezing and coughing. Aches, fever, and a general sense of feeling ill, called *malaise*, are other symptoms. As discussed earlier, some of these symptoms occur because the virus has killed so many epithelial cells; they are discomforts resulting from damage done by the cold virus.

But some common-cold symptoms are not "damage reports." Instead, they are signs that the immune system—the body's disease-fighting machinery—is becoming active against the infection. The next chapter will examine the immune system's response and the ways some cold symptoms are in fact powerful allies in this battle against cold-causing viruses.

•   •   •   •

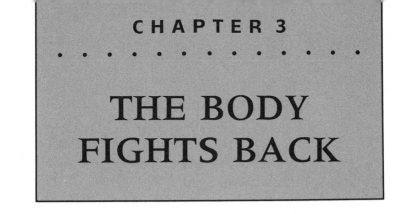

CHAPTER 3

· · · · · · · · · · · · · ·

THE BODY
FIGHTS BACK

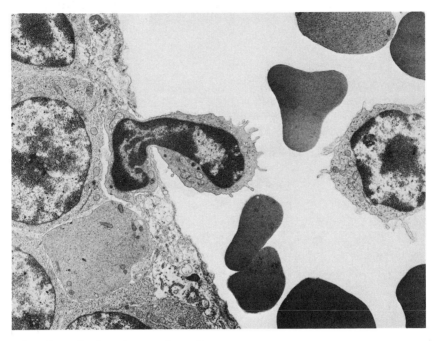

Migration of a lymphocyte from bone marrow.

A few hours after cold viruses invade the human body, a complex and powerful system of defense that is the body's immune system goes into action against them. Scientists do not yet know everything about the immune system, but they do know that it uses many different substances and types of cells to do its disease-fighting work. As they fight infections, the various parts of the immune system also produce many of a cold's unpleasant symptoms.

As early as an hour or so after cold viruses have entered nose or throat cells, the cells begin giving off chemicals called *prostaglandins*. These chemicals cause inflammation (pain, redness, and swelling) at the site of the infection—in the nose, for instance, where they cause feelings of stuffiness and congestion.

Prostaglandins also draw white blood cells called *neutrophils* to battle the invading viruses. (White blood cells are special infection-fighting blood cells.) About two-thirds of all white blood cells in the body are neutrophils. When they reach an area of virus activity, neutrophils engulf and digest any viruses they find outside the target cells. This keeps more cells from being invaded.

Neutrophils also cause further swelling of the infected area, which is uncomfortable for the cold victim. But swelling is an important part of the anti-infection battle, because when swelling occurs, small spaces open up between target cells and the *capillaries* (tiny blood vessels) around them. Then fluid called *plasma* (the clear liquid part of blood) can seep into the spaces. Plasma carries more neutrophils to fight the viruses. Plasma also raises the temperature in target cells. This is crucial because at higher temperatures virus reproduction slows down.

The infected cells also release a substance called *histamine*. This makes blood vessel walls more permeable so that more plasma can seep out of the capillaries. Histamine also causes cells in the nose to secrete more mucus, insuring that if more viruses try to invade they will be trapped in the sticky fluid there. Thus histamine is in part responsible for the runny nose that comes with a cold. This substance also increases pain sensitivity, so it may contribute to the itchy eyes, muscle aches, and sore throat typical of a cold.

If the invading viruses are not too strong or too numerous, the effects of neutrophils and histamine may destroy them all and end the cold. But if many viruses survive, a new stage of the battle begins. Two more kinds of white blood cells, the *monocytes* and *lymphocytes*, join the neutrophils in the antivirus fight.

Monocytes are not very numerous, accounting for only about 5% to 10% of all white blood cells, but they make up for their low numbers by being ferocious infection fighters. Stimulated by inflammation at the infected site, they turn into *macrophages*—

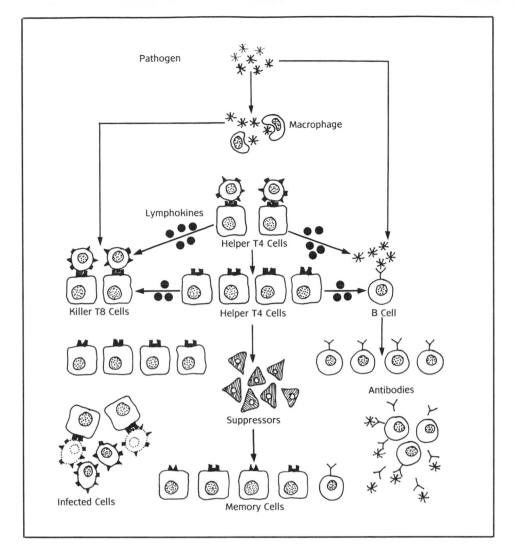

How the Immune System Responds to a Cold Virus Attack. *Macrophages engulf immune system invaders, or pathogens (the virus), then relay their antigenic components (internal components are represented as square; external as triangular) to receptors on T cells. Helper T4 cells then multiply and release lymphokines, which regulate both B and T cells. Interaction with T cells and macrophages motivates the killer T8 cells to mature and roam the bloodstream, destroying the infected cells. At the same time, external antigens on the pathogen interact with B-cell receptors. If the B cells receive signals from the lymphokines, they reproduce antibodies that bind to the antigens, neutralizing them. Suppressor T cells shut down the immune attack, returning the system to normal once the invader is destroyed. Memory cells (antigen-specific) are also created, ensuring that the immune system will more effectively battle the same pathogen in the future.*

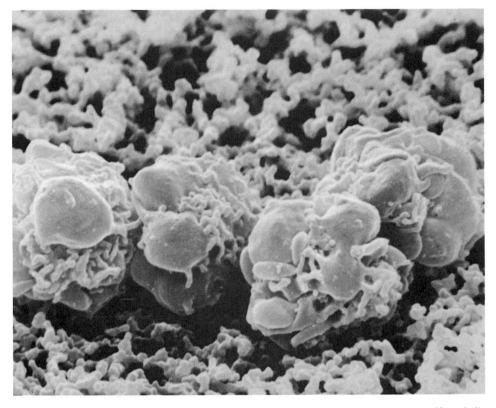

Special white blood cells called neutrophils, pictured here, engulf and digest any viruses they find outside the target cells, thus keeping more cells from being invaded.

a word derived from Greek that means, literally, "big eaters." Macrophages surround and engulf viruses, bacteria, and other foreign matter in a process called *phagocytosis*. Each macrophage can digest 100 virions.

Even more powerful than the macrophages are the lymphocytes, which make up about 25% of the body's white blood cells. When there are no anti-infection battles to fight, the lymphocytes are located in immune-system glands called *lymph glands*. But when activated to battle an infection, they become powerful weapons of the immune system.

One kind of lymphocyte, the *B cell*, develops in *bone marrow* (soft tissue inside bones). Making up about 5% of the body's white blood cells, B cells produce immunoglobulins that attach themselves to viruses, thus preventing the viruses from attaching to target cells. B cells also make immunoglobulins that grab onto the target cells themselves, stopping virus attachment. Some B cells have a kind of memory and can even "remember" viruses that have infected the body before. The "memory" B cells race to the target cells and get there ahead of the viruses, blocking them even more efficiently.

Another kind of lymphocyte, the T cell, is also made in the bone marrow but matures in a gland called the *thymus*. (The thymus is located under the breastbone.) T cells make up 15% to 20% of white blood cells. When the inflammation of an infection signals T cells to become active, the T cells change. Some T cells become killer T cells. These attack infected target cells,

Lymphocytes, shown here, make up 25% of the body's white blood cells. Like neutrophils and monocytes, lymphocytes also fight viral infections.

destroying them before they can release a new crop of viruses. Others become helper T cells, causing B cells to make even more immunoglobulins. Finally, some T cells turn into suppressor T cells. These cells wait until all the viruses have been destroyed, then signal other parts of the immune system to end their activity. This is a vital chore, for without suppressors the immune system would never "turn off," and the body would exhaust itself battling an enemy that no longer existed.

T cells also produce a number of substances that help the immune system fight infections. One is *macrophage activation factor*, which increases the rate at which macrophages engulf and consume viruses. Another, *macrophage migration inhibition factor*, keeps the macrophages in the "battle zone." Yet a third is *interleukin-2*, which causes B cells to produce more immunoglobulins.

Another T-cell product, *interleukin-1*, causes fever. This substance travels in the blood to the brain, which responds by giving the order to "turn up the heat." The body temperature rises, slowing viral reproduction. Higher temperature increases T-cell and B-cell activity, as well. But the body cannot heat up as fast as the brain wants it to, so the brain triggers chills: shivering to warm the body through movement. Although scientists are not sure why, interleukin-1 also breaks down some muscle proteins; thus it is in part responsible for the achiness of a cold.

Finally, T cells produce interferon—the common name for at least 20 different chemical substances used in the immune system. When working against a cold, interferons perform two main chores. First, they spur killer T cells to destroy infected target cells; second, they cause uninfected target cells to make antiviral proteins. Although it is not clear why, cells exposed to antiviral proteins do not let viruses take over. Viruses may invade a protected cell, but they cannot reproduce inside the cell and cannot kill it.

Besides the main substances and cells of the immune system, there are at least 20 "helper" proteins circulating in the body's plasma to work against infections. These proteins attach themselves to viruses so the macrophages can identify and digest them. They also flag infected cells for destruction by killer T cells and perform other chores that help T cells work better. As a group, helper proteins are called the *complement system*.

DEFENSES OF THE RESPIRATORY SYSTEM

Coughing and sneezing are two cold symptoms that are not part of the immune system's battle. Instead, they are among the defenses of the respiratory system. Sneezes occur when hairs in the nose get tickled by a bit of dust, a drop of mucus, or some other irritant. This stimulates nerves that trigger a sneeze automatically. The purpose of a sneeze is simply to get rid of the irritating particle as fast and as forcefully as possible, to ensure that it will not get deeper into the respiratory system where it might block a main air passage.

Coughing is another way of keeping the respiratory system clean. Any particle or small droplet in the trachea or the *upper*

T cells produce interferon, which, in turn, spurs uninfected target cells to produce antiviral proteins.

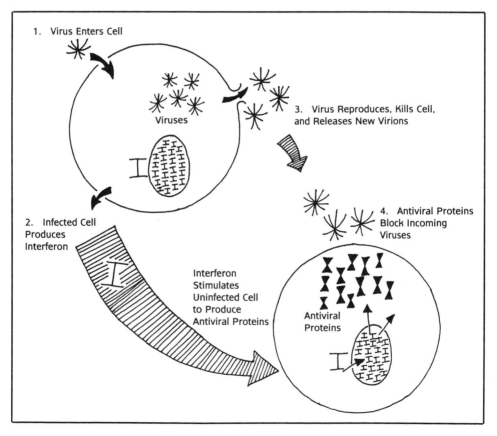

airways (the main air tubes in the upper lungs) irritates nerves in these areas. This triggers the cough, which pushes foreign matter up to the back of the throat where it may be swallowed or spit out.

Coughing is an extremely useful action for cold sufferers. It moves excess mucus out of the lungs before it can thicken and block off the air passages there. Sneezing, on the other hand, is too little, too late. For by the time a cold victim is sneezing, the immune system has already begun responding to a massive cold-virus attack. Thus sneezing is an unpleasant, but not particularly useful, symptom of a cold.

WINNING THE BATTLE

Scientists are not sure just how the immune system finally wins the battle against the cold viruses. Specific answers to the question must await greater knowledge about viruses and about the immune system itself. But in a week or 10 days, the cold begins subsiding. The suppressor T cells signal the end of the battle; fever drops, and the coughing, sneezing, aches, and other cold symptoms gradually ease. Lymphocytes return to the lymph glands; macrophages revert to their normal nonferocious monocyte state; and the whole body goes back to its normal existence.

The cold is over, thanks at least in part to the symptoms that made having it such a miserable experience. Almost all cold symptoms, in fact, come not from the infecting viruses but from the body's powerful immune-system battle against them—a truth that may at least console people the next time they are suffering the symptoms of the common cold.

•   •   •   •

CHAPTER 4

· · · · · · · · · · · · · ·

HOW PEOPLE
CATCH COLDS

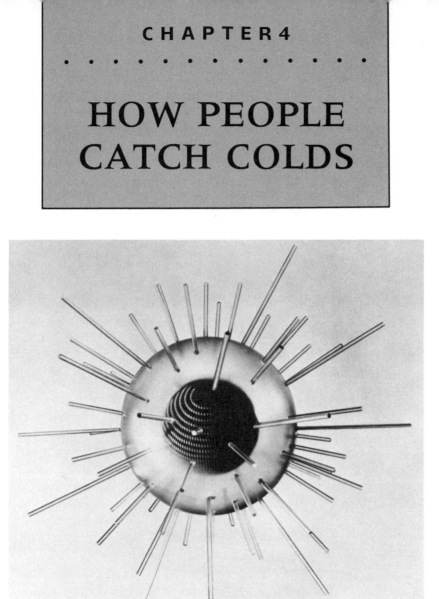

A model of the influenza virus.

For hundreds of years, people covered their mouths when they sneezed, because of superstition: During sneezes, they believed, demons could invade their bodies, or their souls could escape. But after French scientist Louis Pasteur (1822–1895) formulated the germ theory of disease (the idea that tiny organisms caused illnesses), people realized that their superstition had

French chemist Louis Pasteur formulated the germ theory of disease—the idea that microscopic organisms cause illnesses.

a basis in common sense. Covering the mouth trapped germ-carrying droplets expelled by the sneeze, so that others would not breathe them in and become infected.

The idea that colds are spread via droplets from coughs and sneezes is called the aerosol-transmission theory. (An *aerosol* is a cloud or spray of tiny droplets.) The aerosol theory was so widely believed in the early 20th century that during World War I, the British Ministry of Health distributed warning posters: Coughs and Sneezes Spread Diseases—Trap Germs in Your Handkerchief to Keep the Nation Fighting Fit.

Today, scientists still believe some colds are spread via aerosols. The aerosols from coughs and sneezes leave the mouth and nose at speeds of up to 150 miles per hour and remain in the air (because the drops are so tiny) for several hours. Such aerosols seem an excellent method of travel for cold viruses. But the aerosol theory has never been the only theory on the ways colds are spread.

In the 1940s, pioneer British cold-researcher Sir Christopher Andrewes established the Salisbury Common Cold Research Unit, where he tried to find scientific proof of the ways cold viruses spread. Andrewes tried to give people colds by exposing healthy volunteers to the coughs and sneezes of cold victims. But although Andrewes identified cold viruses and grew them in culture dishes—a great success in itself—he could not reliably spread colds by exposing people to virus-laden aerosols. At least some colds, he thought, must be spread in other ways.

Still, the aerosol theory made so much sense that scientists did not want to give it up. After all, everyone "knew" sneezing spread colds—even though it was hard to prove it in the laboratory. In the early 1970s, cold-scientist Robert Couch was ready to try testing the aerosol theory again.

At the National Institutes of Health, Couch put 15 sneezing cold victims in a room along with a dozen healthy volunteers. Between them was only a wire mesh through which aerosols could easily pass. The result: No volunteers caught cold. The study was repeated five times by Couch and others, with similar results. Thus scientists began to think sneezing and coughing might not spread colds, after all. Consequently, they began looking for another form of transmission—one that they *could* prove.

In the late 1970s, Doctors Jack Gwaltney, Jr., and Owen Hendley of the University of Virginia at Charlottesville began testing the idea that colds were spread not by aerosols but by hand-to-hand contact. In their experiments, only 5% of healthy people caught colds when exposed to coughs and sneezes, but a whopping 73% caught them after hand-to-hand contact with cold-sufferers (followed by touching their own nose or tear ducts). The scientists learned also that viruses survive for hours in handkerchiefs as well as on objects such as telephones, dishes, or books.

Gwaltney and Hendley's work changed people's ideas about cold transmission. By the early 1980s, scientists decided that colds were spread mostly by hand-to-nose or hand-to-eye contact, not by aerosols. People who touched objects contaminated with cold viruses carried the viruses to their own eyes or nose by hand.

Then Dr. Elliot Dick of the University of Wisconsin performed still another experiment and reopened the entire controversy. Dr. Dick had sneezing cold-sufferers play cards with healthy volunteers. During the experiment, some people who handled the virus-contaminated playing cards were allowed to touch their nose while others were not. The result: 67% of the volunteers

• • • • • •

What Is Happening Inside the Body
▼

Runny and Stuffy Nose Viruses invade the cells that line the nasal passages and multiply there. This causes irritation, which the body battles with its general-purpose infection-fighting inflammatory response. This causes tissue swelling and extra mucous production.

Sore Throat Throat tissues may become dry and irritated simply from mouth breathing because of a stuffy nose or from coughing. If a viral invasion of the throat is to blame instead, soreness will often be accompanied by swollen glands (which is actually the term given to lymph nodes that enlarge by trapping the virus and fighting off the infection.)

Cough The air passages to the lungs (the trachea and/or the bronchial tubes) become inflamed in response to the virus. A productive cough is usually a good sign—the body is clearing the respiratory tract by loosening the secretions produced as part of the inflammatory response. The nonproductive, or dry cough, on the other hand, is usually due to minor dryness and irritation of the air passageways where the sinuses drain into the throat.

Lung Congestion/Wheezing Thickened secretions—developed in response to the viral infection—are collecting in the bronchial tubes and obstructing air flow.

Chills and Fever The entire body literally heats up to defend itself from the infection by becoming a less hospitable environment for the virus. The accompanying chills or shivers are actually rapid muscle contractions triggered by the hypothalamus, a portion of the brain that regulates body temperature. The slight tremors created by the shivering generate even more heat to thwart the spread of infection.

Dizziness Excess mucus may be blocking the canal that connects the throat to the ear—causing a balance disturbance that produces the sensation of movement even when one is still (vertigo); or fever-induced dehydration may be causing light-headedness.

Headache A virus-induced fever appears to speed up all body function, including the heart rate and blood flow to the head. In addition, the middle ear and sinuses become congested by excess mucus—all of which can result in head pain.

What One Can Do to Relieve Cold Symptoms
▼

Use a properly cleaned vaporizer or humidifier to help thin the secretions so they can be blown away more easily. Blow one's nose with steady, gentle pressure. Forceful blowing can send virus-laden secretions into the canal connecting the nose and ear, which could in turn cause an ear infection.

Gargle with salt water—¼ teaspoon salt, 8 oz. warm water—to soothe irritated tissue.

Use a vaporizer or humidifier and drink fluids or suck on throat drops.

If cough is productive, the best expectorant, or mucus thinner, is hot liquid—such as chicken soup. Also helpful: the moist environment of a steamy shower or room with a humidifier.

Avoid mucus-thickening dairy products such as milk or ice cream.

Drink as much water and juice as comfortably possible. Most of the discomfort attributed to fever—general malaise and occasionally delirium—are actually side effects of dehydration.

Keep one's head as still as possible to keep from becoming dizzy.

See section on how to relieve a stuffy nose. Once congestion is relieved, the head pain should disappear as well.

Reprinted from *Healthfacts,* Center for Consumer Research

Dr. Elliot Dick of the University of Wisconsin conducted an experiment in which sneezing cold-sufferers played cards with healthy people. The test questioned the theory that a cold can be transmitted through nose-hand contact, because none of the healthy volunteers were allowed to touch their noses, and yet many of them caught colds.

who could touch their nose (and so carry viruses there by hand) caught colds—but so did 56% of those who could not touch their nose. Thus in this test, coughs and sneezes spread colds almost as well as they had by hand contact.

Because the results of different experiments have varied so greatly—some supporting the aerosol theory, others demonstrating that viruses are carried by hand, and some showing that both methods work—the question of how cold viruses spread remains unsettled. According to Dr. Gwaltney, "We still don't know how colds spread under natural conditions. Dr. Hendley and I have shown they can be transmitted by hand-to-hand contact. . . . Elliot Dick has established that they can be transmitted by aerosols. It's certainly possible that in the real world, both routes are important."

In other words, one can probably catch some colds from the coughs and sneezes of victims, and others from virus-contaminated objects. Therefore, the route a virus uses to get from one victim to the other very likely depends on the species of virus involved.

VIRUSES AND ROUTES OF TRANSMISSION

Scientists divide the more than 200 known species of cold-causing viruses into 7 main groups. Of these groups, they estimate the following:

- Rhinoviruses cause 30% to 50% of colds and can spread by aerosols and hand-to-hand contact.
- Parainfluenza viruses cause 15% to 25% of colds and are transmitted both by aerosols and hand-to-hand contact.
- Influenza viruses cause 10% to 20% of colds and are spread mostly by aerosols.
- Coronaviruses cause 10% to 20% of colds and may be transmitted through poor hygiene; thorough hand washing after using the toilet may prevent the spread of these colds.
- Coxsackie viruses and echoviruses cause 5% to 10% of colds. Coxsackie viruses are spread efficiently by aerosols; in fact, almost 100% of volunteers exposed to Coxsackie-virus aerosols become infected. Echoviruses may also spread in sewage and are so tough that they can live in chlorinated water; they may also be spread by houseflies.
- Adenoviruses cause 3% to 7% of colds and may spread by aerosols and hand-to-hand contact.

Meanwhile, scientists have not yet identified the causes of as many as 25% of colds, much less discovered their methods of transmission. It may be that some colds are spread in ways not yet known about at all.

SUSCEPTIBILITY

Although it may not yet be possible to predict when a person will catch a cold or to determine how a virus is transmitted, it is possible to identify some people who are more likely to catch colds than others. Perhaps most susceptible are infants, who catch an average of nine colds before the age of one. This is probably because an infant has not had time to become exposed to many germs and so has little natural resistance to colds. Three-year-olds suffer an average of six colds per year, whereas teen-agers have three or four. After that the colds-per-year average drops as a person ages; healthy elderly people have only one or two colds per year.

The reason children get so many colds (aside from the fact that they have not developed much resistance) is probably that they do not practice "polite" methods of coughing, sneezing, or blowing their nose and are in such close contact with one another in day-care centers and schools. Parents and teachers of cold-susceptible children also catch more colds because they are exposed to them so often.

One finding reported in the *Textbook of Pediatric Infectious Diseases* and as yet unexplained by scientists is that before the age of three, boys catch more colds than girls, but after this age females catch more of the infections. Women may be more sus-

Children catch up to six times as many colds as do adults. One reason for this is that children are in such close contact with one another at school or in day-care centers.

ceptible than men because they are often the caretakers of children who have colds. They are particularly likely to catch colds during ovulation (the time during each month when their reproductive system produces eggs), perhaps because of changes in the hormones that their bodies make at this time.

At any age, cigarette smokers tend to have more severe colds than nonsmokers and are more likely to suffer serious complications such as bronchitis and pneumonia. One study reported in the *American Journal of Epidemiology* suggests that smokers catch cold more frequently, too, but other studies do not support this. Children of parents who smoke, however, have been shown to catch more respiratory ailments of all types—not just colds—than children of nonsmokers.

Poor people get more colds than wealthy or middle-income people. This is probably the result of several factors: They live in more crowded places, have more children, have less opportunity to practice good cleanliness habits, have poorer diets, and experience more stress (both physical and emotional) than wealthier people do. All these factors increase their susceptibility to illnesses—including colds.

People of any income group who are in poor general health (inadequate diet, not enough rest or exercise) are more likely candidates for cold viruses. Those who are receiving immune-system suppressing drugs—cancer patients and organ-transplant recipients, for instance—are very susceptible to infections.

People who work or go to school in very dry environments are more susceptible to colds than people who regularly breathe moister air. Air conditioning is a special culprit—it makes people feel more comfortable, but by cooling and drying the air it makes them likelier to catch cold. Cold viruses are more infectious in cold, dry air, in part because dry nasal mucus develops flaws— open spots that let viruses through to the target cells. Low humidity also reduces immunoglobulin production in the epithelial cells of the nose; this means dry air not only lets in more viruses but also lowers immune-system defenses against them once they have entered the body.

Social isolation—a lack of contact with friends, neighbors, relatives, and other people who provide a social framework for a person's life—increases susceptibility to colds. Scientists are not yet entirely sure why this is so; after all, because colds are caught from other people, a lack of contact should protect a person from colds, not increase their frequency. But a 1980 study by Richard Totman, research physician at the Common Cold Research Unit in Salisbury, England, showed that people with fewer social contacts caught more colds and had worse symptoms than people who had more contact with other people.

Similar studies have shown that stressful situations—having to deal with anxieties caused by poverty, injury, divorce, death in the family, and similar problems—also increase the chances that a person will catch cold. Even good events that cause big changes in a person's life—getting a new job, moving, getting into a good school, or making a sports team—can increase stress levels.

Depression—one result of stress and social isolation—has been shown to lower immunoglobulin levels in the body. (Depression is a condition in which people feel sad, hopeless, or helpless over a long period of time.) Studies on stress and isolation suggest that people who live a difficult, lonely life may also have a depressed immune system—one that functions below normal levels and has fewer weapons to battle against colds and other illnesses.

One can reduce his or her susceptibility to colds by practicing good hygiene: by avoiding exposure to coughs and sneezes; by not touching one's eyes and nose; by washing hands after using the toilet and after touching objects that may carry cold viruses; by staying in good general health (diet, rest, and exercise); and by maintaining a social support system—seeing friends, relatives, and others on a regular basis.

•   •   •   •

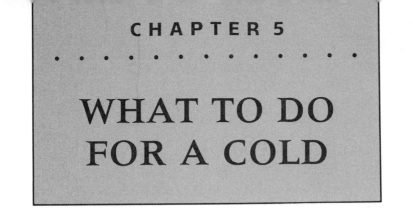

CHAPTER 5

WHAT TO DO
FOR A COLD

An ordinary cold lasts a week or 10 days, and nothing a cold sufferer or doctor can do will shorten it. Antibiotics that work against bacteria cannot halt colds (which are caused not by bacteria but by viruses) and any drug strong enough to stop cold viruses would also injure or even kill the person taking the drug. But there are some cold treatments that help the victim feel better until the cold goes away. The best of these are the old-fashioned home remedies: rest, plenty of fluids, and simple ways of easing discomfort.

Rest is one of the most important treatments for a cold. The "wiped out" feeling of a cold is the body's way of saying it is tired from fighting viruses. Staying in bed for a day or so during the early part of a cold allows the body to rebuild its strength. But it does not really matter where a cold sufferer rests, as long as he or she does so. Staying home during the early part of a cold helps prevent the cold's spread to others, too.

Drinking plenty of fluids is a crucial part of self-treatment during a cold because when suffering from a fever the body uses up a lot of its liquid—especially through perspiration. If this liquid is not replaced, mucus in the nose and lungs dries and thickens, making it hard for the lungs to keep themselves clear. This increases the risk of cold complications, including bronchitis and pneumonia. During a cold, drinking at least eight ounces of hot liquids every two hours helps the body meet its fluid needs, helps ease congestion, and soothes the throat as well.

As mentioned earlier, the most famous and ancient hot liquid ever prescribed against colds—chicken soup—was first recommended by Maimonides 800 years ago. In 1978, to see if the old home remedy had any real effect against a cold, physician Marvin

A nurse at Mount Sinai Medical Center in Miami Beach, Florida, samples some chicken soup. Mount Sinai started manufacturing the soup after one of the hospital's doctors, Marvin Sackner, conducted a study showing that chicken soup clears mucus faster than other liquids.

Sackner of Mount Sinai Hospital in Miami Beach, Florida, tested the effects of hot chicken soup on the clearance of nasal mucus. The faster mucus travels, the sooner it leaves the nose and the less congestion it causes. Writing in the medical journal Chest, Sackner revealed his results in 1978: People who drank cold water had the slowest mucus-clearance rates, hot-water drinkers cleared mucus a bit faster, and those who drank hot chicken soup cleared nasal mucus fastest of all. In short, at least in Sackner's study, hot chicken soup helps.

The chills and fever of a cold indicate that the immune system is geared up and battling the viruses. Keeping warm with a light sweater or blanket helps ease these discomforts, and a cool cloth on the forehead lessens the sensations of fever. (Cold-sufferers who have a fever above 101 degrees Fahrenheit, a fever of 100 degrees lasting more than 2 days, or a fever with a rash, a stiff neck, or a severe headache should consult a physician, because these fevers may signal something more serious than a simple cold.)

The sore throat of a cold may be helped by gargling with warm salt water, taking hot, steamy showers or baths, or using a room humidifier to increase the moisture in the air. Sucking on hard candies or nondrug cough drops may also help, as will drinking hot liquids.

Coughs caused by colds are of two types: productive (bringing up mucus) and nonproductive (dry). For either type of cough, humidity and plenty of hot liquids can help. Coughs that bring up green, brown, or bloody mucus; last more than two weeks; or are accompanied by chest pains, difficulty breathing, or severe chills and fever should be reported to a doctor, for these symptoms may signal a developing pneumonia.

For runny nose and nasal congestion, it is best to use paper tissues for blowing or wiping the nose, because viruses lose potency quickly in tissues but may survive for hours in cloth handkerchiefs. Taking hot baths or showers, drinking hot fluids, and keeping the head elevated may help ease nasal congestion until it goes away on its own.

In addition to these simple cold treatments, there are dozens of cold remedies available in drugstores: over-the-counter drug products that can be bought without a physician's prescription. Each year, Americans spend about $1 billion on these sprays, syrups, capsules, lozenges, and other remedies, and such products often do dry up runny noses, suppress coughs, and stop aches and fever. But the body pays a price when symptoms are eliminated by over-the-counter cold drugs.

The reason is that, as has been shown, cold symptoms are part of the body's fight to cure the cold. No matter how unpleasant the symptoms may be, they are helping the sufferer get well. Also, many over-the-counter cold remedies contain potent ingredients that cause side effects: high blood pressure, fast heartbeat, drowsiness, and other unwanted effects.

Many physicians claim that combination cold remedies—those advertised as relieving all cold symptoms at once—are particularly unwise because they contain several different drugs plus alcohol. Although popular because they are energetically marketed, combination cold remedies are more expensive, more likely to cause side effects, and are no better at easing cold symptoms than simpler, cheaper treatments. No cold-researchers or experts on treating colds have recommended these remedies; the Food and Drug Administration (FDA) 1976 Advisory Panel on Cough, Cold, and Allergy Products did not recommend them, either.

In short, the best drug for a cold is no drug at all, although it is probably unrealistic to think people will avoid drugs entirely. Those who simply must go to work or school while suffering a cold do want to take something that will ease their symptoms so that they can get through the day. For those who feel they need drug-based remedies against the common cold, there are a few comments and cautions.

For easing the chills, fever, and aches and pains of a cold, an over-the-counter drug called acetaminophen is the safest choice. Aspirin should not be taken for a cold. It increases the contagiousness of viral diseases and may decrease immune system action. Also, in those under age 18 who have any viral illness, aspirin has been associated with an increased risk of Reye's syndrome, a potentially fatal disease of the nervous system and liver. Acetaminophen is similar to aspirin but does not produce as many side effects. Available under the brand names Tylenol, Datril, and others, the drug reduces fever and pain when taken strictly as directed by instructions on the package label.

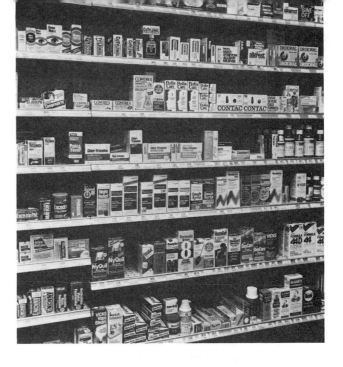

Although over-the-counter cold medicines can relieve symptoms, some of these preparations have unpleasant, even dangerous, side effects.

The FDA approves two categories of drugs for cold-related coughs: cough suppressants and expectorants. Suppressants dull the part of the brain that initiates coughing, and expectorants loosen mucus so that it can be coughed out more easily. A cough lozenge or liquid containing the cough suppressant dextromethorphan is reasonably safe when taken according to label instructions, to stop dry coughing. The main side effect of the drug is drowsiness, so people taking it should not drive or operate machinery; alcohol increases this side effect.

Cough suppressants should not be taken for coughs that bring up mucus, because if coughing does not occur the mucus can thicken and plug up air passages in the lungs. For these coughs, several available expectorants are safe, but the FDA has not judged any of them truly effective. So the best treatment for a productive cough is probably to drink plenty of liquids and forget about over-the-counter cough remedies.

Cough remedies containing a cough suppressant such as dextromethorphan plus an expectorant like turpin hydrate, guaifenesen, or ammonium chloride should be avoided, because suppressing coughs while loosening mucus makes absolutely no sense. Again, as mentioned above, combination cold remedies are best avoided altogether. Sticking to remedies containing just one drug against one symptom keeps drugs from working against one another and lowers the risks of side effects.

Remedies for runny nose and nasal congestion may include antihistamines, anticholinergics, and decongestants, and are available in tablets, syrups, nose drops, and nose sprays. None can be recommended without serious reservations. Of antihistamines, for instance, the FDA reports "insufficient data to establish effectiveness . . . in relieving symptoms of the common cold." That is, they might work, but then again, they might not.

Antihistamines block one of the immune system's antiviral weapons, histamines, and may cause drowsiness, dry mouth, nervousness, and other effects. Thus they may lower the body's disease-curing ability, cause side effects, and may not even ease cold symptoms. Antihistamines found in cold remedies include chlorpheniramine maleate and diphenhydramine hydrochloride.

Anticholinergic drugs that may be ingredients in cold remedies include belladonnine and atropine. They work by blocking the mucus-producing cells in the nose, but because they are extremely potent, they have dangerous side effects. They may soon be banned by the FDA. Their use is not recommended under any circumstances.

Decongestants shrink the tiny blood vessels in the skin inside the nose, thus widening the air passages to relieve stuffiness. In nose sprays, nose drops, pills, or liquids, these drugs may be effective—but they too have major drawbacks. They may cause *rebound congestion*—more swelling than before—as the muscles tightening the blood vessels get tired and sag. They may cause high blood pressure, insomnia, nervousness, or lowered appetite. Also, the tip of a nasal-spray bottle can spread viruses. Thus decongestants should be approached with caution, and nose sprays (if used at all) should never be shared. The FDA-approved decongestants include ephedrine, phenylephrine hydrochloride, racephedrine, pseudoephedrine, and phenylpropanolamine.

Sore throat remedies, by contrast with other over-the-counter cold drugs, are relatively safe. Available as gargles, sprays, or lozenges, they can relieve pain without causing adverse effects. But they should be used only for about two days, because even these remedies may be toxic at high doses and because a sore throat lasting longer merits a medical examination. Approved ingredients in sore throat remedies may include benzocaine and sodium phenolate.

Finally there is vitamin C, a popular cold remedy since 1970, when Nobel Prize–winning scientist Linus Pauling published a book called *Vitamin C and the Common Cold*. In this book, Pauling claimed that very large doses of the vitamin—over 300 times the body's daily requirement—could prevent or shorten the common cold.

Since then, controversy has continued over whether vitamin C is safe in such large doses and whether it works to prevent or cure colds. Even some very reputable scientists disagree on this. Some agree with Pauling; others do not think his tests were done correctly and doubt his results. Until the question is answered one way or another with some certainty, however, it does not seem sensible to take large amounts of a drug that has not been proven safe or effective—especially to treat a fairly mild illness like the common cold.

There are hundreds of other methods people use to treat common colds. They include herbal remedies, homeopathy (a nontraditional type of medicine), acupuncture (using tiny needles to

Dr. Linus Pauling at his 83rd birthday party. In his book Vitamin C and the Common Cold, *Dr. Pauling claims that large doses of vitamin C can prevent or shorten the span of the common cold.*

A family demonstrates "cold chasers"—inhalators believed to cure the cold—at a convention in 1962. Throughout the years there have been many such inventions, but none that has yet "cured" the common cold.

cure disease by releasing blocked energy), hypnosis, and many more. Medical devices against cold symptoms are widely advertised, too; one, called the viralizer, heats the outside of the nose and sends a "medicated" spray into it, thus supposedly destroying cold viruses.

It is not the purpose of this book to detail every possible cold treatment, remedy, or device nor to comment on every treatment method's safety or effectiveness. But a person thinking of trying an over-the-counter cold remedy, an unusual treatment, or a medical device should remember the following facts.

The common cold is an inconvenient but fairly harmless disease. Its symptoms are unpleasant, but they can show that one's immune system is in good shape. And colds go away by themselves in about a week—even with no treatment at all. Meanwhile, all drugs, treatments, and devices have risks and side effects—and none has been scientifically proven to cure colds. Therefore, cold remedies beyond traditional home remedies are rarely called for. They are "treatment worse than the disease"—remedies whose resulting risks and problems may be worse than the cold itself.

It should also be noted that certain groups of people should see their doctors whenever they have a cold. These include children under the age of 10, people older than age 70, pregnant

Pregnant women who contract a cold should visit their doctor for a checkup.

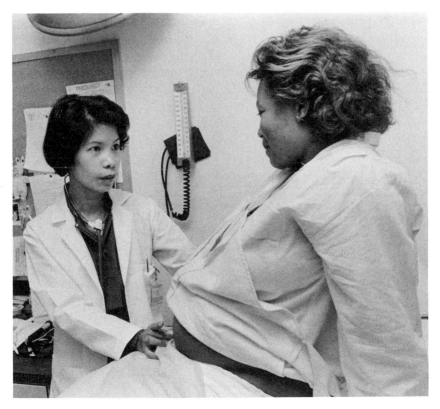

women, and those people who are under a physician's care for other illnesses or allergies. Also, a few cold victims may not get better in a week, or they may develop symptoms such as very high fever, chest pain, or difficulty in breathing. Anyone whose cold does not get better or who develops these more serious symptoms should be examined by a physician immediately. For the rest, the best cold treatments are still rest, plenty of fluids, simple comforts, and perhaps acetaminophen for aches and fever.

•   •   •   •

CHAPTER 6

THE UNCOMMON COMMON COLD

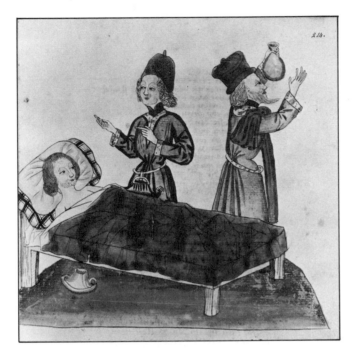

Battling cold viruses uses up some of the immune system's energy. Thus the body may be more apt to get other ailments when it is tired from fighting a cold. When other organisms or infectious agents—bacteria or noncold viruses—take advantage of the tired immune system to cause infection, doctors say that a *superinfection* (infection on top of the original infection) has occurred.

Also, under some conditions cold viruses may get past the body's defenses to infect areas they normally do not penetrate—tissues of the lungs or inner ear, for instance. When cold viruses

Although most colds are harmless and go away by themselves, some do develop into more serious illnesses. Infants and the elderly are most likely to develop such complications.

spread farther and cause more damage than normal, doctors say progression of the *primary* (original) infection has occurred.

Either way, the result may be complications: Instead of getting better, the cold develops into something worse. Babies, elderly people, and people who have general health problems are most likely to develop complications from colds, but even healthy young adults sometimes get them. To reduce the risks of cold complications, it is a good idea to know what they are, how they happen, and what to do if their symptoms occur.

EAR INFECTIONS

Ear infections are the most common complication of colds in children. They begin when swelling blocks a tiny drainage tube leading out of the middle ear. This tube, called the *eustachian tube*, normally drains secretions from the middle ear to the *nasopharynx* (the upper rear part of the mouth cavity).

Blockage of the tube holds fluid deep inside the ear, where bacteria multiply in the trapped fluid. This causes more swelling, more blockage, pressure, and pain. About 70% of ear infections are bacterial, so doctors treat them with antibiotics and a mild pain-relief drug. Ear infections usually clear in a few days, but an untreated ear infection can cause deafness, bone infection, or infection of the spinal cord or brain (meningitis). An earache that lasts longer than a day, gets worse, or is accompanied by fever should be examined by a doctor. Overuse of decongestant nose sprays may cause ear infections by triggering rebound swelling, and forceful nose blowing may push bacteria into the eustachian tubes. Nose sprays should be used with caution, if at all, and nose blowing should be gentle to help prevent cold-caused ear infections.

SINUS INFECTIONS

Sinus infections are also caused by blocked tubes that normally drain secretions into the nasopharynx. The sinuses are hollow, air-filled spaces inside the facial bones, near the nose and eyes. As in ear infections caused by colds, the original difficulty with sinus infections occurs when tissues swollen by cold viruses block normal drainage routes; then bacteria infect the fluid trapped in the sinuses. The result is pain directly above or below one or both eyes, on the sides of the nose near the eyes, or deep inside the head. Applying a heating pad or hot washcloth to the painful area often eases the pain of blocked sinuses, but pain that does not respond to home remedies should be treated by a doctor because antibiotics may be needed against bacterial sinus infections. Decongestant nose sprays and forceful nose blowing may cause sinus infections the same way they cause ear infections and should be avoided to help prevent these troublesome cold complications.

TONSILLITIS

Tonsillitis is an infection of the tonsils, which are made of lymph tissue and located on either side of the upper throat. The tonsils are part of the immune system; their job is to capture viruses or bacteria in the mouth and throat in order to keep them from causing infections. But sometimes the tonsils are overrun with disease organisms and become infected themselves, causing a sore throat and fever. The glands may become so swollen in babies and children that they block the eustachian tubes and cause an ear infection, too. A very sore, swollen throat that hurts during swallowing may be a symptom of tonsillitis. At one time, infected tonsils were routinely removed by surgery called tonsillectomy. In the 1950s and 1960s, about 1 million children per year had their tonsils out. Today, doctors treat the ailment with antibiotics (because many tonsil infections are bacterial) and with mild pain relievers such as acetaminophen.

BRONCHITIS

Bronchitis is an infection of the larger air passages in the lungs. It can be a complication of colds in smokers, people with allergies, and those exposed to chemical fumes or dust at work. Its

Colds can lead to ear or sinus infections, bronchitis (an infection of the larger air passages of the lungs), or pneumonia (an infection of the tissues in the lungs).

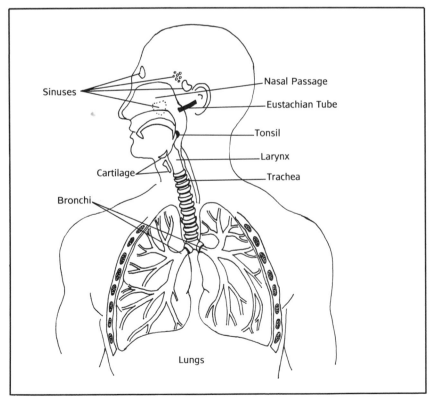

Five young brothers enjoy a bowl of ice cream after having their tonsils removed in 1960. At one time, infected tonsils were routinely removed. Today, most doctors treat tonsillitis with antibiotics.

main symptom is a lingering cough, sometimes accompanied by a fever. The cough may produce mucus, or it may be dry and hacking. Bacteria or viruses may cause bronchitis, or it may simply be an irritation left over from the original cold.

The best way to get rid of bronchitis is to stop smoking and avoid other lung irritants such as exposure to dust and fumes. A bronchitis that does not clear on its own—for example, if the cough continues for more than two weeks after the cold ends—should be treated by a doctor; if bacteria are the cause, the disease may respond to antibiotics. Repeated bouts of bronchitis, continued smoking, or ongoing exposure to lung irritants can lead to chronic bronchitis. In this condition, the cough does not go away and the lungs may be seriously damaged. Chronic bronchitis sufferers are also more likely to get pneumonia.

PNEUMONIA

Pneumonia is an infection of the tissues in the lungs, specifically of the tiniest air passages and the air sacs where oxygen passes into the blood. It may be very serious and even fatal. A cold can lead to pneumonia if the immune system fails to keep cold viruses from invading lung tissue or if mucus produced during the cold is not effectively coughed out. Or bacteria may invade the lungs while the immune system is busy fighting cold viruses.

The symptoms of pneumonia are sharp chest pain, cough (worse than the cold's cough), intense chills, and a dramatically high fever—sometimes as high as 105 degrees Fahrenheit. Sometimes the victim also experiences nausea and vomiting. In some cases, the victim's cough produces a green, yellow, brown, rust-colored, or bloody mucus.

Victims of pneumonia should seek medical attention immediately, because the disease can progress very quickly. Treatment of pneumonia depends on its cause. Bacterial pneumonias are treated with antibiotics, which must be taken for about two weeks even though the worst of the symptoms subside sooner. Antibiotics do not work against viral pneumonias, so the treatment involves rest, fluids, oxygen for breathing difficulty, and medications to reduce pain and keep fever within a safe range (extremely high fevers can cause brain damage). Even after the symptoms ease, a person who has had pneumonia should rest and take especially good care of him- or herself to avoid suffering a relapse (another bout of pneumonia).

ASTHMA

Asthma, a condition in which the small air passages in the lungs constrict so that it is hard to breathe, is not usually the result of a cold, but it can be triggered when the cold's extra mucus irritates the air passages. A cold sufferer who develops *wheezing* (a whistling sound during breathing) or who has difficulty breathing should see a physician. People who know they have asthma should be alert for an attack while they have a cold. Asthma is treated with drugs to ease spasms that squeeze the airways in the lungs.

BRONCHIOLITIS

In infants, bronchiolitis is an infection of the small air passages in the lungs. It is caused by a virus called respiratory syncytial virus (RSV). Because infants' air passages are so tiny, the swelling caused by RSV can block their air. The symptoms of bronchiolitis are fast breathing, fever, anxiety, and difficulty in drawing breath;

the baby's chest may "suck in" during inhalation because the effort is so great. In the past, the only treatment for bronchiolitis was humidity; parents used vaporizers to fill the room with water mist or sat in the bathroom with the child while the shower ran hot to increase the humidity in the air. Today, there is a drug called ribaivarin, marketed under the brand name Virazole, that works against respiratory syncytial virus. Ribaivarin is available only by a doctor's order, works only against RSV (as far as doctors now know), and is one of the only known effective antiviral drugs developed to date.

COLD SORES

Cold sores—red, crusty, painful lesions on the lips—sometimes develop during or after a cold or the flu. They are caused by the herpes simplex virus type 1 (HSV-1). By age 14, about 70% of Americans have been exposed to the virus, but only a few get cold sores; it is not known why some people develop them around the time they have colds. Herpes simplex virus type 1 is contagious while the open sores are present, so people who have them should avoid kissing others and be especially careful about their cleanliness habits until the sores are completely healed. This usually takes 7 to 10 days. Some physicians recommend an ice pack on the developing cold sore because cold may block the sore from "blooming." For cold sores that keep coming back, a physician may prescribe cream containing the drug acyclovir. This drug, like ribaivarin, is an antiviral—one of the very few such agents yet developed. It is effective only against herpesviruses (both 1 and 2) and is only available by a physician's prescription.

OTHER ILLNESSES

Some diseases with coldlike symptoms are not colds. The most common of these is influenza, or flu. Influenza is caused by influenza and parainfluenza viruses. An illness characterized by a cough, runny nose, fever, achiness, and a general "rotten feeling" that comes on suddenly instead of a bit at a time may be flu instead of a cold. Flu viruses tend to infect a lot of people at once, so when many people in a school or other community fall ill around the same time, flu is likely to be the culprit. In practice, it does not make much difference whether a person has a cold or the flu, because the treatment for either disease is the same: rest, drinking plenty of fluids, and simple methods of reducing discomfort. Influenza, like the common cold, goes away in 7 to 10 days. The complications of flu are much like those of the common cold.

A sore throat that seems worse than the one usually accompanying a cold may be strep throat—a throat infection caused by Streptococcus bacteria. In this disease the other signs of a cold may be present, but the sore throat is the worst symptom the victim feels. Antibiotics work against the bacteria causing strep throat, so an unusually severe sore throat should be examined by a doctor. Usually, the doctor will do a throat culture. Then the right antibiotic can be prescribed.

Some allergies imitate colds, too. They can cause coughing, sneezing, sore throats, runny noses, achiness, and even fevers. People who know they have allergies are experts at deciding whether they have colds or allergies at any given time, because they can feel the small differences between the symptoms. But some allergies strike people who have never had them before, so colds that do not seem normal should be checked by a doctor to rule out allergies.

Finally, many common diseases of childhood and young adulthood—measles, mumps, chicken pox, scarlet fever, and mononucleosis, among others—may begin or continue with symptoms very much like cold symptoms. A coldlike illness accompanied by swollen glands in the neck or elsewhere, or by a rash, very high fever, blurred vision, stiff neck, yellowed eyes or skin, darkened urine, pain when urinating, or any other unusual symptoms should be seen by a physician.

To sum up: Most colds run their course in 7 to 10 days. It is important to rest, drink plenty of fluids, and take good care of oneself while the cold is present to avoid complications. Many of a cold's complications can be treated effectively by a doctor. If a cold is accompanied by symptoms other than a simple cough, runny nose, sore throat, mild fever, and fairly mild malaise, a doctor should be consulted without delay. If a cold lasts longer than a week or 10 days, a doctor should be consulted, too.

•   •   •   •

CHAPTER 7

PREVENTING COLDS

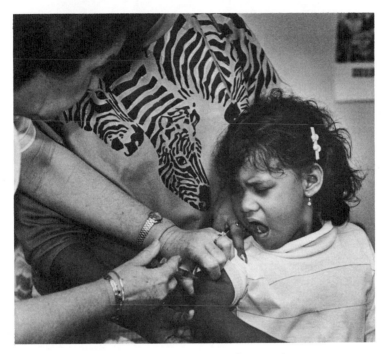

A young girl receives an injected measles vaccine.

One weapon modern medicine can wield against many virus-caused diseases is vaccination. A vaccine is a substance that stimulates the immune system to make antibodies against a particular disease germ. Vaccines have been developed against smallpox, measles, mumps, and other very serious illnesses—but not against colds. To understand why, it may help to know about another vaccine that has been successful: the Sabin polio vaccine.

73

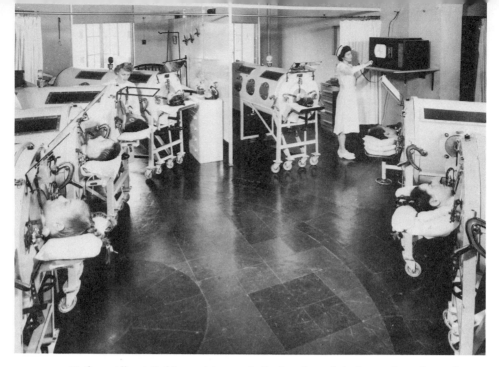

Before Albert Sabin and Jonas Salk developed their vaccines for polio, many victims of the disease were encased in iron lungs (mechanical respirators).

In 1916, the first great polio epidemic hit the United States, killing or paralyzing many of its 30,000 victims. More "waves" of the illness followed, so that by 1940 there were hundreds of thousands of polio-crippled survivors: some in wheelchairs, some who could only hobble in metal leg braces, many encased in iron lungs—huge devices that pumped air in and out of the lungs of victims who were too weak even to breathe for themselves.

Doctors and scientists already knew the cause of the disease: poliovirus. They also knew that polio was incurable. So their only hope to save future victims lay in preventing the disease. To achieve this, they knew, they had to develop a vaccine against polio.

By the late 1940s, scientists had discovered that only three types of poliovirus were causing disease. This meant a vaccine only had to work against the three related viruses, not against many viruses. They also found that people who got mild cases of polio were safe from later attacks; once the body made antibodies against polio, a person was immune for life. And they knew that, at least in their laboratories, polioviruses could be killed or weakened, to make them safe for use in a vaccine. (Vaccines are often made from such denatured or killed viruses.)

By 1954, two American scientists—Albert Sabin and Jonas Salk—had developed two very different vaccines. Salk's vaccine used viruses that had been killed and was given to more than 500,000 children in 44 states between 1953 and April 1955. Sabin, meanwhile, continued to work on his vaccine, which used live but weakened polio viruses.

Then came tragic news: The Salk vaccine protected most children from polio—but in some, it caused the disease. One hundred and fifty children were paralyzed and 11 died from the effects of the Salk vaccine, which was at once withdrawn for further safety improvements.

Sabin was convinced that his own vaccine was not only more effective but safer, and by 1957 he had tested it on 10,000 monkeys and on hundreds of volunteer prison inmates. But he had not tested it on those who needed the vaccine most: children. Sabin worried that in children the vaccine might cause tragic side effects, as the Salk vaccine had.

Finally, however, Sabin tried his vaccine on his own daughters and on his wife. Fortunately, it worked and did not infect them. The Soviet Union then invited Sabin to test his vaccine on 4.5

Dr. Jonas Salk was one of the first scientists to develop a polio vaccine. Although his preparation protected most of the children he innoculated, it caused the disease in others.

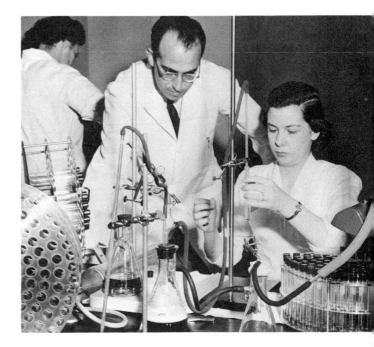

Biologist Michael Rossman of Purdue University works on a model of the common-cold virus. Rossman, along with colleague Ronald Ruckert of the University of Wisconsin, discovered why it is so difficult to develop a successful cold vaccine—because the cold virus has the ability to change its shape.

million Russian citizens. The vaccine worked on the Russian citizens as well and on 200,000 people in a vaccine-testing program in Cincinnati, Ohio. By 1960, more than 100 million people had received the Sabin polio vaccination. Albert Sabin's vaccine ended polio epidemics everywhere it was used, reducing the illness by 99% all over the world and dropping the number of U.S. cases to 20 or fewer per year.

The polio vaccine success story illustrates the four reasons why similar success has not been achieved against the common cold. First, polio was caused by 3 viruses; colds are caused by more than 200. So whereas a polio vaccine was hard to make, creating a cold vaccine is all the more difficult. In 1985, in fact, virus researchers Michael Rossman of Purdue University and Ronald Ruckert of the University of Wisconsin found that making a cold vaccine may be even more difficult than had been thought. They fed all the known facts about a cold virus called RV-14 into a computer. The computer created a diagram of the virus, which looked like a 20-sided polyhedron. But then it turned out that the virus could *change* its shape, which means a vaccine would have to work against many viruses *and* against all their possible forms. This hugely increased the problems of developing a cold vaccine.

The second difference between creating a polio vaccine and a cold vaccine is that polio was a crippling or fatal disease; consequently, scientists working against it received a lot of financial support. By contrast, colds are relatively mild ailments, so it is difficult to raise as much money for research against them.

Third, once the body has antibodies against polio, it will keep them for life. But antibodies against cold viruses last only a few years, at most. For them to be as effective, a way to get the body to make long-lasting cold antibodies would have to be found— and science has not yet progressed far enough to do that.

Finally, polio was so dangerous that the risk of a new vaccine was less than the risk of letting people continue unvaccinated. Even the fact that early vaccines caused some cases of polio was not as bad as doing nothing and thus allowing thousands more to die. By contrast, cold victims suffer mildly and then get well. It makes little sense to take the risk of trying new vaccines on people just to prevent mild ills such as the common cold.

In short, no vaccine against colds is likely to be available in the near future. But scientists are working on other possible ways to prevent colds. One way, developed by cold-researcher Elliot Dick, is the *virucidal* (virus-killing) tissue. Quite simply, the virucidal tissue is a Kleenex brand tissue soaked in citric acid, malic acid, and sodium lauryl sulfate—a combination of chemicals that kills both cold and flu viruses on contact.

In 1985, Elliot Dick tested the tissues and found they reduced colds by more than 75% in people who used them. The makers of Kleenex, Kimberly-Clark, marketed the tissues under the brand name Avert in several big cities. But not many people bought the tissues, because they cost three times as much as plain Kleenex and because news of how well they worked had not been spread effectively. The company plans to try selling the tissues again but has not yet announced when.

Experiments by biologist Albert P. Krueger at the University of California at Berkeley suggest that plenty of fresh air may prevent colds. He studied air *molecules* (a molecule is composed of one or more atoms and is the smallest possible particle of a substance that retains that substance's properties) called ions. An ion is a molecule that has a tiny electrical charge, much too small to feel. Molecules of fresh air have negative charges; stale, polluted, or smoky air molecules have positive charges.

In one study, a machine to make negatively charged air ions was placed in a bank office, while another office did not receive

A healthy diet—eating the right foods in the right amounts—can help a person fight off disease more effectively.

a machine. Over time, the illness rate among employees in the two offices was measured. The result: People in the positive-ion ("indoor air") office had significantly more colds than those in the negative-ion ("fresh air") atmosphere. Krueger suggests that positive ions may prevent colds by altering levels of *serotonin*, a chemical the body uses in many of its functions, including the working of its immune system.

Reducing stress levels may also help prevent colds by increasing body levels of immunoglobulin A, some forms of which fight cold viruses. In one study, researcher R. C. Green of Harvard University measured levels of immunoglobulin A in healthy volunteers. He found that after 20 minutes of relaxing with eyes closed, people's immunoglobulin A levels increased significantly.

As mentioned earlier, some people think that taking large amounts of vitamin C can help prevent or cure colds. But the vitamin's effectiveness on colds has not been completely proved. Scientists also do not know what long-term side effects large doses of the vitamin may cause. So it may be wiser not to take big doses of vitamin C in the hope of preventing colds—at least until science offers proof of its safety and effectiveness.

Even without special virus-killing tissues, air ions, or relaxation techniques—and without unproven drugs—it is possible to reduce one's likelihood of catching colds by developing some basic health habits. These habits fall into four simple categories: nutrition, rest, exercise, and cleanliness.

Good nutrition—eating the right foods in the right amounts—gives the body the energy and the raw material it needs to fight off diseases more effectively.

Regular exercise—walking, playing sports, or any other activities that make the body work hard—helps build up the body. When viruses strike, a strong body is better than a weak body.

Rest is important to prevent colds and other illnesses because rest times are the times when the body can rejuvenate itself. Rest means giving the body, mind, and emotions a break—so they

Regular exercise helps build up the body, making it stronger and more able to fight off a cold.

can come back more strongly against viruses or any other disease challenges.

Cleanliness is an important method of preventing all kinds of diseases, including the common cold. Washing hands often, avoiding the coughs and sneezes of people who have colds, and keeping food, dishes, clothes, and bodies clean can stop cold viruses—as well as other disease germs—from reaching your body and infecting it.

●   ●   ●   ●

CHAPTER 8

A COLD-FREE TOMORROW?

Dr. Guy Diana of Sterling Winthrop Research Institute.

For most people, colds are mild illnesses. But for some, they can be extremely dangerous. Victims of immune-system diseases such as AIDS, cancer patients whose immune systems are weakened by medicines and therapies, and people who have other serious ailments can suffer serious effects from colds and even die of them. Anticold treatments that carry risk or discomfort make more sense for such victims than they do for healthy persons.

One cold treatment now being developed for people whom colds may seriously harm is zinc, a mineral the body needs in very tiny amounts when it is well. In the first small clinical trial of zinc (involving 146 people) at the University of Texas in 1984, cold-sufferers who let zinc tablets dissolve in their mouths got rid of their colds several days sooner than those who did not use zinc.

At first, scientists thought the zinc stopped cold viruses from multiplying. But University of Virginia cold-researchers Felicia Geist and Judith Bateman tried zinc against viruses in test tubes and found it did not stop virus multiplication. Thus scientists now think zinc may work directly on the immune system, boosting its activity.

According to the first developer of the zinc cold lozenge, George Eby of the University of Texas, a major drug company is testing zinc for use in a cold medicine. Eby also said that he thinks the drug may be available by the early 1990s. But he would not say which drug company is testing zinc, and no drug company has asked the FDA for permission to do any more tests. It may be too soon to get excited about zinc, because FDA-approved testing takes a long time—usually at least seven years.

Also, zinc has serious side effects at fairly low doses. Nausea, vomiting, damage to blood cells, and a general sensation of feeling poorly are the results of taking too much zinc. So even if this mineral is approved for use against colds, its discomforts and dangers may restrict its use to those for whom colds pose real health threats.

Interferons, a group of substances that the immune system produces to increase its attacks against viruses, were first thought to be a possible cold cure in 1957. But it was so difficult and expensive to make interferons in laboratories that scientists initially gave up the idea of using them as medicine. In the late 1970s, however, a new technique called *genetic engineering* made interferons easier and cheaper to produce.

In genetic engineering, scientists take the gene for interferon production from an appropriate cell (a gene is a section of a cell's

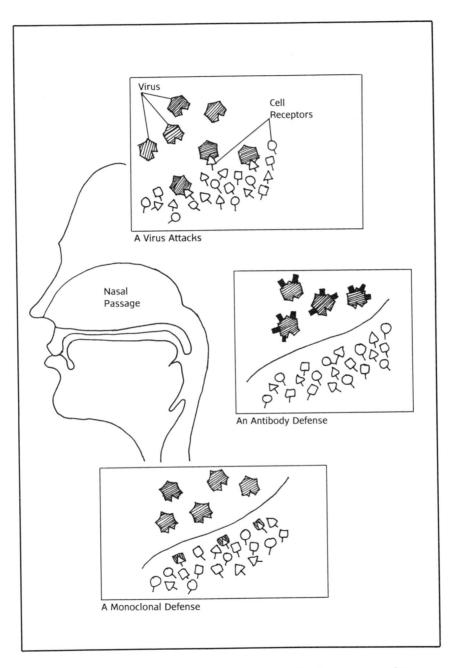

Monoclonal antibodies work by binding to a particular receptor site, thereby changing its shape and preventing the virus from binding to it.

DNA that codes for a specific trait) and put it into another cell—one they can grow in large numbers in the laboratory. Thus they can create large populations of interferon-making cells and harvest plenty of interferon.

By 1986, interferons were shown to reduce colds by 30% or 40% when used by healthy people who were exposed to cold viruses. The users took the interferon in the form of a nose spray—an easy method of treatment. And only 12% of users had side effects: runny nose, congestion, and similar symptoms. Thus the Schering-Plough Corporation, a large drug-manufacturing company, has asked the FDA to approve the interferon nose spray under the brand name Intron.

But interferons are not a perfect cold cure for the general public. First, they are expensive: The amount needed to prevent one cold costs $245. Second, Intron would be available only by a doctor's prescription because interferons are powerful substances that could have unknown side effects on the immune system. Finally, because getting FDA approval can take years, interferons will not be available at all until at least the mid-1990s, if then. This is because many more tests must be done to make sure interferons are safe and effective enough for people to use.

Another drug, called WIN 51,711, is being tested by Sterling Winthrop Research Institute. The drug attaches itself to cold viruses and prevents them from invading nose and throat cells. It has been shown to work against viruses in test tubes and in some laboratory animals, but no tests in human beings have yet been done. Thus even if WIN 51,711 turns out to be safe and effective against colds, it will not be available for several more years—again because of FDA test requirements.

Yet another development in possible future cold cures is represented by genetically engineered proteins called monoclonal antibodies. These are substances that block viruses from attaching to receptor sites, the spots viruses use to "hang on to" cells that they are infecting. If a monoclonal antibody fills a cell's receptor site, the virus cannot fit there—and therefore cannot infect it.

Drug scientist Richard J. Colonno of the Merck Sharp & Dohme drug company has found that cold viruses use only two receptors on each nose and throat cell. In 1984, he located one of the receptors and developed a monoclonal antibody to block it. By 1986, he had found the second site and had begun work on an antibody to block it, too. The work, however, is difficult and slow; Colonno said he hopes to have some kind of progress to report by 1990. And even when both monoclonal antibodies have been developed, they must block every single virus-attachment site on every epithelial cell in the nose and throat to be effective. So final development of a monoclonal-antibody cold cure or preventive will take a long time, and there is no guarantee it will ever be completely successful.

Research on zinc, interferons, and monoclonal antibodies may eventually do much more than fight colds. Such work also increases knowledge about noncold viruses and about the immune system in general. This is just the sort of knowledge that is needed to fight serious, even life-threatening ailments that are much

The AIDS virus. Research regarding the common cold is unlocking the secrets of the human immune system and may someday lead to medical breakthroughs in the fields of cancer and AIDS research.

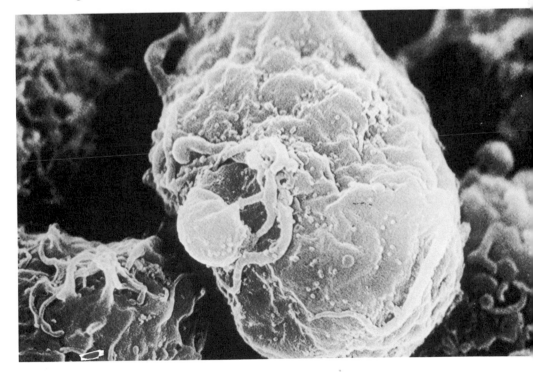

worse than the common cold. Interferons, for instance, are being tried against some forms of cancer; monoclonal antibodies might be used not only against colds but against many other viral diseases as well.

Right now, prospects for cure or prevention of the common cold are uncertain. By the time today's young people are raising families, better methods against colds may be available. Meanwhile young people and their families can take comfort in knowing that an ordinary cold will go away by itself and that treatment for cold complications is safer, more effective, and more available than at any time in history.

•   •   •   •

EPILOGUE

· · · · · · · · · · · · · · · ·

COMPLICATIONS
OF SMOKING

Most people fight off a cold in about a week, suffering from no further complications and resuming their everyday work. But some people find it harder to recover from colds. Their body's defense systems may be weakened or damaged and, consequently, may not be quick enough or able to respond to the harmful invader.

One group of people who have particular trouble getting rid of colds are smokers. Cigarette smoke causes the bronchial cilia to beat more slowly—thus slowing down the mucus-cilia transport system that carries foreign particles out of the body. This gives bacteria the opportunity to remain in the body and multiply. As a result, smokers suffer from more upper respiratory infections than nonsmokers.

Not only does smoking allow bacteria to build up in the body, but it does a great deal of damage in and of itself as well. Cigarette smoke, the particles of which are too small to be caught in the mucus, bypasses the lungs' defense system. Consequently, its toxic gases and particles enter the body, stimulating goblet cells to produce extra mucus, which further slows down the cilia. This extra mucus can plug up airways and serve as the perfect breeding ground for bacteria. Smoking also cripples macrophages, which are then unable to dispose of the foreign matter that has collected in the mucus and airways.

In addition to all of this, smoke carries in it small particles of matter—little bits of sticky tar—that enter the respiratory system. These invaders force the lungs to secrete enzymes to neutralize them. These enzymes damage—and can eventually destroy—the lung tissue.

All of this damage to the respiratory system does more than prolong colds. If they are unable to clear their lungs of excess mucus and fluids, smokers may fall prey to a host of other illnesses and diseases, including pneumonia or bronchitis. Smoking may also trigger asthma attacks, which, if not treated promptly and adequately, can prove fatal.

Emphysema is a disease known almost exclusively among smokers. In fact, an estimated 90% of those people suffering from the disease are, or once were, heavy smokers. When a person suffers from emphysema, his or her lungs produce excessive amounts of mucus and the alveoli (the lungs' air sacs) lose their elasticity, getting loose and baggy. It becomes more and more difficult for the body to exhale, and air becomes trapped in the lungs, overexpanding them. Over a period of time, the walls of the lungs begin to disintegrate and the lungs can no longer efficiently move air or transport oxygen and carbon dioxide. The heart, in an effort to make up for the lungs' shortcomings, pumps harder. Eventually, the heart will sustain permanent damage.

Symptoms of emphysema include a chronic cough, followed by shortness of breath, which worsens until the person is hardly able to breathe at all. Most emphysema patients must carry portable oxygen tanks in order to breathe and function at all. If the patient stops smoking at an early point, the lungs will partially repair some of the damage. If the patient continues smoking, or if the disease has progressed very far, death is the eventual consequence.

In addition to emphysema, 300,000 deaths occur each year as a result of lung cancer. An estimated 83% of these deaths are believed to be smoking related. For people who begin smoking at a young age, the chances of developing one of these fatal diseases are great. Naturally, the best defense against this is to stop smoking or, better yet, never start at all. For although some teenagers believe that the worse consequence they face if they smoke is a lingering cold, in reality the long-term effects are far more grave indeed.

•   •   •   •

APPENDIX 1:
IS IT A COLD OR THE FLU?

The following chart lists the symptoms of both the common cold and the flu. Although there are some symptoms that appear with both illnesses (a cough, for example), for the most part the symptoms vary, even if only by degree. As with the common cold, if flu symptoms worsen or persist for more than a week without letting up, consult a physician.

Symptoms	Cold	Flu
Fever	Rare	Characteristic High (102°−4° F); sudden onset; lasts 3−4 days
Headache	Rare	Prominent
General aches and pains	Slight	Usual; often quite severe
Fatigue and weakness	Quite mild	Extreme; can last 2−3 weeks
Prostration	Never	Early and prominent
Runny, stuffy nose	Common	Sometimes
Sneezing	Usual	Sometimes
Sore throat	Common	Sometimes
Chest discomfort, cough	Mild to moderate; hacking cough	Common; can become severe
Source: National Institute of Allergy and Infectious Diseases		

APPENDIX 2:
VIRAL DISEASES

Viral Disease	Major Target Organ(s)	Major Mode of Transmission	Major Portal of Entry
Measles	Respiratory tract and skin	Respiratory droplets	Respiratory tract
Mumps	Respiratory tract salivary glands, and nervous system	Respiratory droplets and saliva	Respiratory tract
Influenza	Respiratory tract	Respiratory droplets	Respiratory tract
Common cold	Respiratory tract	Respiratory droplets	Respiratory tract
Smallpox	Skin, mucous membrane, liver, spleen, and lungs	Respiratory droplets	Respiratory tract
Chickenpox	Skin and occasionally lungs	Respiratory droplets	Respiratory tract
Herpes simplex Type 1	Buccal mucosa	Contact	Mucous membrane of mouth
Herpex simplex Type 2	Genitals	Sexual contact	Mucous membrane of genitals
Poliomyelitis	Gastrointestinal tract and nervous system	Feces (and fecally contaminated food or water)	Alimentary tract
Rabies	Nervous system	Saliva	Wound, usually an animal bite
Hepatitis A	Gastrointestinal tract, liver, and spleen	Feces (and fecally contaminated food, water, or fomites)	Alimentary tract
Hepatitis B	Liver	Infected blood; occasionally feces, urine, semen, and respiratory secretions	Parenteral mucous membranes and alimentary tract

APPENDIX 3:
FOR MORE INFORMATION

The following is a list of organizations and associations that can provide further information on the common cold, diseases that are related to or can develop from the common cold, and the immune system in general. For further information regarding local organizations and treatment centers, please refer to the appendixes in the ENCYCLOPEDIA OF HEALTH volumes *Allergies* and *The Immune System*.

ALLERGY

American Academy of Allergy and
 Immunology
611 East Wells Street
Milwaukee, WI 53202
(414) 272-6071

American Association for Clinical
 Immunology and Allergy
311 Oakridge Court
Bellevue, NE 68005
(402) 292-8950

National Institute of Allergy and
 Infectious Diseases (NIAID/NIH)
9000 Rockville Pike
Building 31, Room 7A32
Bethesda, MD 20892
(301) 496-5717

ASTHMA

National Jewish Hospital/National
 Asthma Center
3800 East Colfax Avenue
Denver, CO 80206
(303) 398-1565

IMMUNOLOGY

Histamine Research Society of
 North America
c/o Timothy Sullivan, M.D.
Department of Internal Medicine
 and Microbiology
University of Texas Health Science
 Center
5323 Harry Hines Blvd.
Dallas, TX 75235
(414) 276-6445

International Organization of
 Allergology and Clinical
 Immunology
350 Sparks Street, Suite 602
Ottawa, Ontario K1R 7S8
Canada
(613) 238-8120

RELATED DISEASES

American Broncho-Esophagological
 Association
200 First Street SW
Rochester, MN 55905
(507) 284-4348

American Lung Association
National Headquarters
1740 Broadway
New York, NY 10019
(212) 315-8700

Canadian Lung Association
75 Albert Street, Suite 908
Ottawa, Ontario K1P 5E7
Canada
(613) 237-1208

Lung hot line: (800) 222-LUNG
Colorado: (303) 398-1477

National Reye's Syndrome
  Foundation (NRSF)
426 North Lewis
Bryan, OH 43506
(419) 636-2679

The following organizations can provide more general information on the common cold and related diseases.

Alliance for the Prudent Use of
  Antibiotics (APUA)
P.O. Box 1372
Boston, MA 02117
(617) 956-6765

American Medical Association
  (AMA)
535 North Dearborn Street
Chicago, IL 60610
(312) 645-5000

American Pediatric Society
c/o David Goldring, M.D.
500 South Kings Highway
St. Louis, MO 63110
(314) 367-6880

Canadian Pediatric Society
Centre Hospitalier Universitaire de
  Sherbrooke

Sherbrooke, Quebec J1H 5N4
Canada
(819) 563-9844

Centers for Disease Control
Department of Health and Human
  Services
Public Inquiries
Building I, Room B63
1600 Clifton Road NE
Atlanta, GA 30333
(404) 329-3534
(800) 342-7514

National Foundation for Infectious
  Diseases (NFID)
P.O. Box 42022
Washington, DC 20015
(301) 656-0003

FURTHER READING

Alexander, Dale. *The Common Cold and Common Sense*. New York: Fireside, 1971.

Bennet, Hal Z. *Cold Comfort: Everybody's Guide to Self-Treatment*. New York: Potter, 1979.

Castleman, Michael. *Cold Cures*. New York: Fawcett, 1987.

Desowitz, Robert S. *The Thorn in the Starfish: How the Immune System Works*. New York: Norton, 1988.

Dick, Elliot. "Interruption of Transmission of Rhino Virus Colds Among Human Volunteers Using Virucidal Paper Handkerchiefs." *Journal of Infectious Diseases* 153 (February 1986): 352–56.

Eron, Carol. *The Virus That Ate Cannibals*. New York: Macmillan, 1981.

Feigin, Ralph D., and James D. Cherry. *Textbook of Periodic Infectious Diseases*. Philadelphia: Saunders, 1987.

Green, R. G. "Immuno-Enhancement: A Comparison of Four Relaxation Methods." *Psychosomatic Medicine* 48 (March/April 1986): 304.

Journal of the American Medical Association. "Medical News" (column), January 17, 1986, 301–6.

Krueger, Albert P., and E. J. Reed. "The Biological Impact of Air Ions." *Science* 193 (September 24, 1976): 1209–13.

Locke, David. *The Smallest Enemy*. New York: Crown, 1974.

Mizel, Steven B., and Peter Jaret. *The Human Immune System*. New York: Fireside, 1985.

Monto, A. S., et al. "Relation of Acute Infections to Smoking, Lung Function and Chronic Symptoms." *American Journal of Epidemiology* 107 (January 1978): 57–64.

Murphy, Wendy. *Coping with the Common Cold*. Alexandria, VA: Time-Life, 1981.

Pauling, Linus. *Vitamin C and the Common Cold*. New York: Freeman, 1970.

Roberts, Carl R., James D. Turner, M.D., et al. "Reducing Physician Visits for Colds Through Consumer Education." *Journal of the American Medical Association* 250 (October 21, 1983): 1986–89.

Sackner, Marvin. "The Effect of Respiratory Drugs on Mucociliary Clearance." *Chest* 73 (July 1978): 958–66.

Tapley, Donald F., et al., eds. *The Columbia University College of Physicians and Surgeons Complete Home Medical Guide*. New York: Crown, 1985.

Zimmerman, David R. *The Essential Guide to Non-Prescription Drugs*. New York: Harper & Row, 1983.

"Zinc and Colds." *Science News* 130 (October 11, 1986): 238.

PICTURE CREDITS

GLOSSARY

acetaminophen a drug similar to aspirin, used for treatment of pain and fever

acetylsalicylic acid aspirin

acupuncture a method of treating disease that involves inserting needles into specific points on the body

adenovirus a cold-causing virus that may be spread by aerosols and by hand-to-hand contact

aerosol a fine mist composed of tiny droplets

aerosol transmission theory the idea that colds are spread by way of droplets from coughs and sneezes

AIDS acquired immune deficiency syndrome; an acquired defect in the immune system, thought to be caused by a virus (HIV) and spread by blood or sexual contact; leaves people vulnerable to certain, often fatal, infections and cancers

antibiotics drugs, produced by or derived from a microorganism, that work with the body's immune system to inhibit the growth of, or destroy, bacteria and to cure illness

antibody one of several types of proteins, produced by the body, that reacts against bacteria, viruses, and other foreign matter

anticholinergics drugs that block the mucus-producing cells in the nose; these drugs include belladonna and atropine

antihistamine a substance that blocks the body's production of histamine

B cell also called B lymphocytes; a type of white blood cell that helps fight infections

bacterium a unicellular, microscopic organism that lacks a distinct nuclear membrane; many but not all bacteria cause disease

bone marrow the soft tissue inside bones

bronchitis infection or inflammation of the air tubes in the lungs

capillaries tiny blood vessels that connect arteries and larger vessels

capsid the outer coat of a virus

catarrh a cold, especially with a runny nose

cilia tiny hairs

complement system a complex series of blood proteins whose action "complements" the work of antibodies; complement proteins destroy bacteria, produce inflammation, and regulate immune reactions

coronavirus a cold-causing virus that is spread in unsanitary conditions

Coxsackie virus a cold-causing virus that is nearly always spread by aerosols

decongestant a substance that reduces swelling in the nose and large air tubes of the lungs

DNA deoxyribonucleic acid; a nucleic acid that is found in genes and is a carrier of hereditary information

echovirus a cold-causing virus that may be spread by houseflies

epidemic an infectious disease that affects many people at one time in the same area

eustachian tube a connecting passage between the inner ear and the upper-rear portion of the nose

expectorant a substance that loosens mucus in the air tubes of the lungs so it may be coughed out

flaws open spots in dry nasal mucus that let viruses through to the skin

genetic engineering the science of altering or transferring hereditary information

germ theory of disease the idea, formulated by Louis Pasteur, that tiny organisms cause illness

histamine a substance that causes allergic responses; produced by the body in response to injury, irritation, or infection

homeopathy a method of treating disease that involves giving a patient a small dose of a drug that would normally cause the symptoms that the patient is having

immune system the organs, tissues, cells, chemicals, and responses used by the body to fight off infection or invasion by bacteria, viruses, and other foreign matter

immunoglobin a type of protein produced by the immune system to act as an antibody and help fight infection

inflammation redness, swelling, heat, and pain caused by an injury or infection

influenza a cold-causing virus, spread mostly by aerosols

interferon one of a group of substances that help cells defend themselves against viruses and other infections

interleukin-1 a T-cell product that causes fever by traveling in the blood to the brain, which responds by increasing body temperature

leeching a method of relieving colds in ancient Greece by cutting the victim or applying blood-sucking leeches to remove blood and excess fluids from the body

lymphocyte a type of white blood cell involved in immunity; includes B cells and T cells

lysis cell death caused by damage from viruses

lysogeny the process by which a virus reproduces inside a cell by forcing the cell to replicate the virus's DNA along with the cell's own DNA

macrophage a type of white blood cell that engulfs and digests viruses and other infectious agents or organisms

malaise a general feeling of illness

monoclonal antibody a laboratory-made antibody that blocks a virus from fitting into an attachment spot on a cell, stopping the virus from infecting the cell

monocyte a large phagocytic white blood cell; in the presence of infection, monocytes turn into macrophages

mucus the heavy, thick liquid that forms a protective coating over bodily channels

narcotic a habit-forming drug that dulls the senses, relieves pain, and induces sleep

nasopharynx the upper-back portion of the throat, directly behind the nose

neutrophil an abundant, phagocytic type of white blood cell that helps fight infection

nostrum a medicine with secret ingredients and usually doubtful effectiveness

parasite an organism that takes all it needs to live from other organisms

plasma the clear, liquid part of the blood

pneumonia an infection of the tissues in the lungs

prostaglandin a chemical produced by the body in response to injury, infection, and for numerous other reasons

respiratory system the organs and tissues that the body uses to breathe

Reye's syndrome a potentially fatal disease of the nervous system and liver, linked to the use of aspirin in people under 18 years of age

rhinovirus one of the many viruses that can cause the common cold in humans

ribosomes structures inside cells that aid in protein formation

salicylic acid an acid used to make aspirin

sinuses hollow spaces in the bones of the face near the eyes and nose

superinfection a second infection by a different germ, especially one that occurs when the body is weakened by the first infection

symptom an unwell feeling, abnormal appearance, or inability to function properly that signifies the presence of disease

T cell also called T lymphocytes; a type of white blood cell that helps fight infection by signaling other lymphocytes to attack invading cells or chemical structures foreign to the body

temperate able to infect without causing damage

thymus gland where the T cells grow, located under the breastbone

tonsillectomy surgery in which tonsils are removed

tonsillitis an infection of the tonsils

toxin a poison produced by a living creature

trachea the main air tube leading into the lungs

transmission the spreading of a disease

turbinates flaplike ridges in the nose that help warm and moisten air that is breathed in

vaccine a substance that causes the body to make antibodies to fight a disease germ

viralizer a medical device that heats the outside of the nose and sends a medicated spray into it, with the aim of killing cold viruses

virions complete viral particles; created when a virus incorporates its DNA into that of an invaded cell, forcing the cell to reproduce the virus

virulent tending to cause disease

virus a tiny infectious agent that invades cells in order to reproduce

vitamin C a vitamin found in plants, fruits, and vegetables; believed by some scientists to be effective against colds

white blood cells special blood cells that fight infection

INDEX

Mary Kittredge, a former associate editor of the medical journal *Respiratory Care*, is a free-lance writer of fiction and nonfiction. She is certified as a respiratory-care technician by the American Association for Respiratory Therapy and has been a member of the respiratory-care staff at Yale–New Haven Hospital and Medical Center since 1972.

Ms. Kittredge was educated at Trinity College, Hartford, and the University of California Medical Center, San Francisco. She is the author of *The Respiratory System, Prescription and Over-the-Counter Drugs, Organ Transplants*, and *Headaches* in the Chelsea House ENCYCLOPEDIA OF HEALTH and of young adult biographies of Marc Antony, Frederick the Great, and Jane Addams. Her writing awards include the Ruell Crompton Tuttle Essay Prize and the Mystery Writers of America Robert L. Fish Award for best first short-mystery fiction of 1986.

Dale C. Garell, M.D., is medical director of California Children Services, Department of Health Services, County of Los Angeles. He is also associate dean for curriculum at the University of Southern California School of Medicine and clinical professor in the Department of Pediatrics & Family Medicine at the University of Southern California School of Medicine. From 1963 to 1974, he was medical director of the Division of Adolescent Medicine at Children's Hospital in Los Angeles. Dr. Garell has served as president of the Society for Adolescent Medicine, chairman of the youth committee of the American Academy of Pediatrics, and as a forum member of the White House Conference on Children (1970) and White House Conference on Youth (1971). He has also been a member of the editorial board of the *American Journal of Diseases of Children*.

C. Everett Koop, M.D., Sc.D., is Surgeon General, Deputy Assistant Secretary for Health, and Director of the Office of International Health of the U. S. Public Health Service. A pediatric surgeon with an international reputation, he was previously surgeon-in-chief of Children's Hospital of Philadelphia and professor of pediatric surgery and pediatrics at the University of Pennsylvania. Dr. Koop is the author of more than 175 articles and books on the practice of medicine. He has served as surgery editor of the *Journal of Clinical Pediatrics* and editor-in-chief of the *Journal of Pediatric Surgery*. Dr. Koop has received nine honorary degrees and numerous other awards, including the Denis Brown Gold Medal of the British Association of Pediatric Surgeons, the William E. Ladd Gold Medal of the American Academy of Pediatrics, and the Copernicus Medal of the Surgical Society of Poland. He is a Chevalier of the French Legion of Honor and a member of the Royal College of Surgeons, London.